CENTRE FOR EDUCATIONAL RESEARCH AND INNOVATION
NATIONAL CENTER ON ADULT LITERACY (NCAL)

D1798603

Learning to Bridge
the Digital Divide

B 1 313137 0

OECD

ORGANISATION FOR ECONOMIC CO-OPERATION AND DEVELOPMENT

ORGANISATION FOR ECONOMIC CO-OPERATION AND DEVELOPMENT

Pursuant to Article 1 of the Convention signed in Paris on 14th December 1960, and which came into force on 30th September 1961, the Organisation for Economic Co-operation and Development (OECD) shall promote policies designed:

- to achieve the highest sustainable economic growth and employment and a rising standard of living in Member countries, while maintaining financial stability, and thus to contribute to the development of the world economy;
- to contribute to sound economic expansion in Member as well as non-member countries in the process of economic development; and
- to contribute to the expansion of world trade on a multilateral, non-discriminatory basis in accordance with international obligations.

The original Member countries of the OECD are Austria, Belgium, Canada, Denmark, France, Germany, Greece, Iceland, Ireland, Italy, Luxembourg, the Netherlands, Norway, Portugal, Spain, Sweden, Switzerland, Turkey, the United Kingdom and the United States. The following countries became Members subsequently through accession at the dates indicated hereafter: Japan (28th April 1964), Finland (28th January 1969), Australia (7th June 1971), New Zealand (29th May 1973), Mexico (18th May 1994), the Czech Republic (21st December 1995), Hungary (7th May 1996), Poland (22nd November 1996) and Korea (12th December 1996). The Commission of the European Communities takes part in the work of the OECD (Article 13 of the OECD Convention).

The Centre for Educational Research and Innovation was created in June 1968 by the Council of the Organisation for Economic Co-operation and Development and all Member countries of the OECD are participants.

The main objectives of the Centre are as follows:

- *analyse and develop research, innovation and key indicators in current and emerging education and learning issues, and their links to other sectors of policy;*
- *explore forward-looking coherent approaches to education and learning in the context of national and international cultural, social and economic change; and*
- *facilitate practical co-operation among Member countries and, where relevant, with non-member countries, in order to seek solutions and exchange views of educational problems of common interest.*

The Centre functions within the Organisation for Economic Co-operation and Development in accordance with the decisions of the Council of the Organisation, under the authority of the Secretary-General. It is supervised by a Governing Board composed of one national expert in its field of competence from each of the countries participating in its programme of work.

FOREWORD

As we enter the 21st century, the emerging features of the "New Economy" can be seen everywhere. At the heart of these changes are the innovations made possible by Information and Communication Technology (ICT), which are transforming the ways in which economies, and the people within them, are working. ICT has become one of the main drivers of growth, but economic growth, important as it is, must be promoted in tandem with social and democratic objectives, especially in tackling exclusion. The risk for some of being disconnected through being unable to participate in the modern economy is now acute, with participation conditional to a large extent on accessing ICT with confidence and competence. This is increasingly the condition for involvement in the decision-making and community activities that also define participation in society.

The importance of ICT to both economic and social development explains the priority of bridging what has come to be known as the "digital divide". This is, in fact, a whole series of interlocking "divides" - the gaps that separate segments of society as well as whole nations into those who are able to take advantage of the new ICT opportunities and those who are not. "Crossing the digital divide is essential for being competitive", as expressed in the *2000: A Better World for All* report we have just produced with the IMF, the UN, and the World Bank Group. This critical importance was affirmed by the G8 leaders at their Okinawa Summit in Japan last month, when they agreed to set up a "Digital Opportunity Task Force" as a matter of urgency.

People, education and learning lie at the heart of these issues and their solutions. The machines and sophisticated ICT equipment are useless without the competence to exploit them. Nurturing this competence is in part the job of schools and colleges, where the foundations of lifelong learning and "technological literacy" are laid. In part, it is dependent on the learning that takes place throughout life in homes, communities, and workplaces. Education and learning are now the lifeblood of our 21st century knowledge societies, and ICT has become integral to them. The gaps that define the "learning digital divide" become as important as the more obvious gaps in access to the technology itself.

OECD will continue to be a pathfinder in the analysis of ICT and its policy implications. This volume, based on a recent conference we organised jointly with the National Center on Adult Literacy (NCAL) in the US, could not be more timely. It contains analysis of problems, and promising policy initiatives to overcome them, for both OECD and non-OECD countries. It indicates the global importance of education and lifelong learning to ensure that the positive gains of digital diversity and opportunity replace the exclusion of the digital divide.

Donald J. Johnston
Secretary-General of the OECD

August 2000

ACKNOWLEDGMENTS

This publication builds on the papers and discussions of the Fifth NCAL/ OECD Roundtable[1] organised at the U.S. National Center on Adult Literacy (NCAL), University of Pennsylvania, 8-10 December 1999. The Roundtable, entitled *The Lifelong Learning and New Technologies Gap: Reaching the Disadvantaged*, was attended by around 60 participants from OECD and non-OECD countries. Co-sponsors were the Office of Vocational and Adult Education (OVAE) in the U.S. Department of Education, UNESCO, the IBM Corporation and the International Literacy Institute.

The organisers are grateful to all who participated in the Roundtable and would like to acknowledge in particular those who presented the thematic papers, which were subsequently revised for publication: Nolan Bowie, Lynda Ginsberg, Guillermo Kelley-Salinas, Sten Ljungdahl, John Sabatini, Richard L. Venezky, and Daniel A. Wagner. Acknowledgements are also due to those participants who prepared for the Roundtable written documentation relating to ICT and

---

1. The first was held in 1993; publications from the earlier Roundtables are: Hirsch, D. and Wagner, D.A. (1994), *What Makes Workers Learn? – The Role of Incentives in Workplace Education and Training*; Tuijnman, A., Kirsch, I. and Wagner, D.A. (eds.) (1997), *Adult Basic Skills: Innovations in Measurement and Policy Analysis*; Stern, D. and Wagner, D.A. (eds.) (1996), *International Perspectives on the School-to-Work Transition* (all published by Cresskill, NJ: Hampton Press); OECD (1996), *Adult Learning and Technology in OECD Countries*, Paris.

the learning digital divide in their country, extracts from five of which have been included in Chapter 9. In addition, the respondents to the theme papers made a valuable contribution – Wadi Haddad, Knowledge Enterprise, Inc., U.S.A.; Ronald Pugsley, OVAE; Jan Visser, UNESCO; and Ingrid Volkmer, University of Augsburg, Germany. Stephen McNair, University of Surrey, U.K., himself a respondent during the Roundtable, worked in close co-operation with the OECD Secretariat to prepare the "policy overview" introductory chapter of this volume.

The principal Roundtable organisers were NCAL Director Daniel Wagner, with his colleagues Marilyn Liljestrand and Kelly Limeul, and Edwyn James of the OECD/CERI Secretariat. The report was prepared by Edwyn James and David Istance of the CERI Secretariat, assisted by NCAL and OECD colleagues.

TABLE OF CONTENTS

CHAPTER 1
THE EMERGING POLICY AGENDA
by
Stephen McNair[2]

INTRODUCTION: UNDERSTANDING THE DIGITAL DIVIDE

As digital technologies become firmly embedded in everyday affairs, they enable most people to lead more productive and rewarding lives. They can help all societies to solve long standing economic and social problems, but they also bring new challenges. Those denied access to ICT skills and knowledge become less-and-less capable of participating in an economy and a society that are increasingly technology-dependent. The resulting *digital divide* represents a major challenge to policy-makers at all levels. What should governments do? What *can* governments do, to ensure that the new technologies do not consign some people to the margins of society, unable to contribute to and benefit from the wealth of new opportunities that the digitally rich enjoy?

The examples in this report confirm that, used wisely, the technologies themselves can be a powerful influence in the lifelong learning context, in helping to overcome the inequalities in society. Those alluded to briefly in this chapter are to be found more fully developed later. They show, however, a clear risk that

2. Professor, University of Surrey, United Kingdom.

without policy intervention, ICT will intensify societal divisions rather than close them. Easy access to ICT enables people to become richer, and therefore more able to afford still newer technology; it is, moreover, the already well educated who – disproportionately – take up lifelong learning opportunities and who, in general, get better services. In short, the educated *information rich* become richer and the less educated *information poor* become poorer.

Just as the industrial revolution made some level of literacy and numeracy a requirement for all, so the electronic revolution within contemporary society makes *digital literacy* essential. People who lack access to relevant hardware and software, and a basic understanding of ICT, will also lack the confidence that they can continue to learn as the technologies evolve; they will remain *digitally illiterate*. As the technologies become ever more embedded in everyday life – and increasingly taken for granted by those with relevant equipment, skills and understanding – so the exclusion of those without this new *literacy* deepens. Such exclusion is a major policy concern in all countries. It poses a dynamic problem, in that the very concept of ICT literacy is itself constantly changing as new technologies emerge.

There are many technologies undergoing rapid and unpredictable change, constantly offering increased capacity and new techniques. In five years, for example, the World Wide Web has moved from being an eccentric interest of enthusiasts to become a major tool of economic and cultural activity. The linking of mobile communications technology and computing is likely to bring access to communities without reliable electricity or telephone services (or with none at all), while digital television will soon deliver Internet access to anyone with a television set. Such volatility makes investment decisions risky for governments, accustomed as they are to more stable environments.

While obtaining physical access to hardware and software is a problem for many, the access is not an end in itself. It is useful only in so far as it helps people to address the challenges which face them as individuals, citizens and employees. The technology is of no benefit without the skills and understanding to make use of it, to achieve purposes relevant to the individual's circumstances and needs. There is a complex and dynamic relationship between acquiring the skills and putting the technology to use, since ICT offers the opportunity to do old tasks better and to undertake tasks never before contemplated.

All is not, however, inherently benign. The unregulated market is likely to develop ICT to address the needs of the better educated, wealthier and more technology-literate individuals, communities and countries, since these are the people who will want and be prepared to pay for the development of new and more sophisticated products and services. Policy-makers are thus faced with a double challenge: how to ensure that all citizens have equitable access to the equipment and the skills needed to participate, and how to ensure continuous updating as new technologies and applications emerge. This report illustrates the high commitments and expectations across many countries – along with the serious levels of concern – as access to digital technologies is extended or contemplated. OECD governments cannot ignore the challenge of the digital divide.

TECHNOLOGY AND EXCLUSION

There is a growing agreement across OECD countries that, even leaving aside the compelling moral arguments, modern economies cannot afford a significant uneducated and excluded minority. As the report recounts,[3] exclusion reduces the capacity of individuals to contribute to – and benefit from – society and the economy. It increases the costs which the unwilling majority have to bear, while sowing the seeds of civil and political instability.

Exclusion is a complex phenomenon involving many causes, of which limited education is one, and in contemporary society lack of access to current technologies another. The various factors interact with each other at local, national and global levels, in changing and sometimes unpredictable ways. Whole communities and countries may be excluded on account of historical, cultural and economic forces; the gulf between technology-rich and technology-poor countries and continents may be as stark as that between local communities and individuals. To some extent, the digital divide is simply a deepening of existing forms of exclusion. Those who are unemployed, poor, housebound, disabled, less educated, members of cultural and ethnic minorities – and in many countries, women – are all likely to have restricted access to digital technologies, just as they are less likely to have access to other services and goods. The same is true for those whose mobility is restricted by domestic circumstances or who are in prison, and for those living in communities which are geographically isolated, or dependent on declining industries.

Examples are documented in this report of ICT helping to overcome some forms of exclusion. The Mexican Telesecundaria programme[4] shows that ICT

---

3. See, for instance, Chapter 9.

4. See Chapter 2 for the examples in the next two paragraphs.

can provide ways of delivering services where staff are not available or are too expensive. It can make it easier for people in isolated locations – whether in a remote community in Northern Canada or housebound in a high rise city apartment – to participate in social and economic activity. Some of the benefits are surprising. The technologies can enable whole countries to leap stages of economic development which took centuries in Europe. Thailand's *Project Lighthouse* seeks to make the transition directly from a pre-industrial to a post-industrial economy in a few years, while the absence of a legacy of old telecommunications systems in Botswana has enabled them *ab initio* to install a leading-edge infrastructure.

One of the great strengths of the technologies lies in their ability to serve many purposes. The computer used as a workstation in working hours can be a learning station outside. The laptop on which a community group keeps its accounts can also be loaned to members to undertake their own learning activities. The LINCOS project demonstrates the benefits and potential savings which come from providing technology-based access to education, medicine and public information for remote communities in Costa Rica.

However, not all problems of exclusion are susceptible to technological solution: the costs may be daunting, especially given the need for continuing updating, and the economies overstated. Furthermore, the human issues are complex. The technology may be seductive, diverting resources from more effective but less glamorous issues of developing human skills. English is the dominant language of the Internet, arguably therefore imposing a whole range of values on smaller cultures and linguistic diversity. Even so, the example of Maori education in New Zealand[5] demonstrates that digital technologies can support minority cultures and languages, and benefit can come as language communities across the globe are linked electronically. More subtle effects also arise. Women are less likely than men to be users of both the digital technologies and lifelong learning, but there are exceptions. Furthermore, there is concern in some developed countries about the exclusion of young working class men, faced with declining traditional industries, who see desk work – and therefore work with computers – as not appropriate for men.

TECHNOLOGIES AND LIFELONG LEARNING

Digital technologies are both a subject – something to learn about – and a tool to assist learning in general. They also change what can be known and

---

5. See Chapter 7.

learned, by making new kinds and quantities of knowledge available and open to debate. Applied in the workplace and the political arena, they transform economic, social and political processes, creating still further learning needs as they do so. They can also transform how, where and when learning takes place. The rise of digital technologies is therefore one of the most powerful determinants in lifelong learning, since communities and individuals who lack confidence in handling these new tools will be at an increasing disadvantage in a global market and society.

This is to present governments with three distinct (and expensive) policy issues: how to ensure that young people are prepared for this world; how to ensure that adults who have already completed their formal education are enabled to participate in it; and how to ensure that everyone is able to continue to update skills and understanding, as the technologies and the social and economic environments change. The concept of lifelong learning has entered the conventional rhetoric of the policy community in most OECD countries, but remains much misunderstood. National policy-makers are accustomed to thinking of education as pertaining to children and young adults, largely in public sector institutions. Such formal education is a central part of lifelong learning, but much learning happens outside the framework of public sector institutions, through the involvement of parents, employers, commercial agencies and voluntary organisations, often with different structures, principles and values.

Lifelong learning calls for a paradigm shift, asking what is most effectively learned when, and how the resources of individuals, firms, communities and the state are best deployed across a life-span. This implies not only a major expansion in the volume of learning activity but a new relationship between learner and provider. Where it is clearly proper for the state to determine the framework of formal schooling for its citizens – though with due consultation – in later life the agenda is set by individuals, employers and communities, reflecting their own priorities and ambitions. National policies must come to terms with a new and unfamiliar political dynamic, in which governments facilitate and encourage, with limited powers of direction.

Formal schooling lays the foundations for later learning and for participation in society and the economy. Governments are working in a volatile environment, to define what all school leavers ought to be able to understand and do in relation to digital technologies, and to find the necessary resources.[6] They are also working

---

6. See Chapter 8.

to put in place infrastructures to underpin development, such as digital networks and portals like Sweden's Schoolnet and the UK's National Grid for Learning. Digital technologies themselves are making a growing contribution to this phase of education, enriching and sometimes replacing conventional processes, providing cheap access to a diversity of information, allowing interactivity and individualised learning experiences on a scale never previously possible.

Formal initial education is a vital element of the policy agenda. Although it represents less than a quarter of the average life-span, it is a period largely devoted to learning. Much lifelong learning is not bounded by institutional forms, and learners cannot be expected to define themselves conveniently as *higher education students* or *work-based learners.* They are as likely to turn to a book, a commercial distance-learning product, a workmate or neighbour, as to a public sector institution. The Swedish report stresses the importance of voluntary groups and trades unions as providers of learning. Recent research in the UK (Coffield, 1998), has confirmed that most of the important learning for industrial workers happens in and around the workplace, not on training courses or under formal supervision. For such lifelong learning, notions of *teaching* and *classroom* do not apply. What matters is how the workplace and the community are organised to make learning a natural and inevitable part of everyday life, not something done in a special place.

It would be a mistake, however, to see formal and informal learning as two entirely separate worlds. A lifelong approach implies examining them together, and there can be powerful synergies between them, across the generations. For adults with literacy problems, one of the powerful motivators to return to learning is the need to keep up with their own children as they begin schooling. An example is the New Zealand Maori education project where young people were only allowed to attend ICT classes if they brought an adult learner with them.[7] For those already motivated to learn, digital technologies offer learning opportunities previously inaccessible. The technologies can help to articulate previously unexpressed needs, and provide services tailored specifically to the individual. They may offer more acceptable modes of learning, for instance to those who prefer the privacy of learning with a computer to the public stresses of the classroom. On the other hand, they can support community-based learning, which becomes more sustainable through the support that individuals bring to each other.

---

7. Illustrations for the remaining paragraphs in this section are drawn from Chapters 6-8.

Digital technologies also change the role of the teacher and our understanding of learning processes. They give learners direct access to vast bodies of knowledge, as well as tools to analyse and search for material. Well used, they enable learners to engage more directly with the subject, through interactive systems, virtual experiments and networking with other learners and practitioners. The skills of finding and interpreting information are seen to be more important than the skills of retention and recording, which is particularly helpful for adults who come to learning in order to solve particular problems in their lives, work or community. For them, desirable learning is based not on a teacher's notion of a coherent body of knowledge but on fitness for purpose.

However, this radical shift in the role of the teacher, described as the move from "the sage on the stage" to "the guide on the side", can be very threatening to teachers educated in a very different tradition. Not all governments have recognised the urgency and scale of the issue, though the report offers some illustrative strategies to tackle it. Sweden and Finland have a commitment to the formal retraining of teachers (itself an aspect of lifelong learning), while the UK's National Grid for Learning seeks to provide underpinning support for teachers. The *Captured Wisdom* project is a radical development, in which teachers are linked electronically to observe each others' work, creating a virtual community of practice to share ideas and develop confidence in new and unfamiliar roles.

A lifelong, technology-supported model of education also challenges traditional forms of educational institution, as we move from an emphasis on buildings, students, and teachers and textbooks as knowledge providers, to a knowledge infrastructure, learners, tutor/facilitators and multimedia materials. Lifelong learning implies greater diversity of need and learning approaches, which digital technologies allow – software can build personal profiles of each user, to map progress, to tailor approaches and to offer challenges matched to individual needs. Furthermore, the technologies enable the growth of global online providers, making resources available to learners at any time and location, and leaping the national boundaries within which education policy and management has traditionally been conducted. A key policy issue here is how far the traditional institutional frameworks can adapt to this new world, and how far we must develop new kinds of institution and structure to address them.

Finally, a lifelong perspective raises questions about the balance between individual and communal learning. Although formal schooling is usually conducted in groups, it normally assesses and values individual prowess. Much lifelong learning, however, has a collective focus. In a working or community context, the priority is what the team, workgroup or firm can achieve, using the talents of all its members. The technologies make some such learning easier – software can allow a group of people to contribute to the same task, to discuss problems, and to offer and receive advice. In the report a range of approaches to communal learning is identified, including community/government partnerships in Mexico. In the UK's laptop initiative, community groups are invited by government to present proposals for a community need which they could meet with a laptop computer. Those whose bids are successful are provided with a machine, and with software and networked support enabling the learning of digital skills to be embedded in the activity of the group, rather than added on as a tutorial course.

POLICY INTER-RELATIONSHIPS

The relationships between ICT and lifelong learning, on one hand, and the broad common policy objectives of all OECD governments – to improve economic competitiveness and reduce social exclusion – are complex. The figure below illustrates the complexity. There are policy initiatives which support both competitiveness and inclusion, and there are ways of using digital technologies which support lifelong learning. The focus of most contributors to this report lies in the centre of the diagram, where lifelong learning and digital technologies come together to support both policy objectives. If we are to overcome the digital divide, it is important to increase the size of this area.

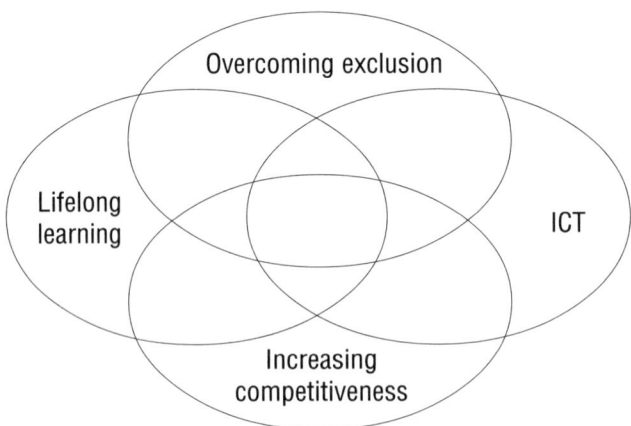

For policy-makers, the key questions are always: what *should* be done and what *can* be done? For this report, both questions are critical. The large-scale advent of ICT changes the political processes through which policy is formed, and the extent to which government can control it. Issues arise at all levels. The divide between the information rich and information poor exists between individuals in the same neighbourhood, as well as between nations and continents. Whether one argues from natural justice, political stability or economic efficiency, the digital divide has to be addressed. Hence the call within this volume for some form of global solidarity in the development of access to ICT and to lifelong learning.

THE POLICY AGENDA

There are at least eight key areas for government to consider, in relation to the changing world of ICT, in order that individuals and communities are not excluded from participation in society and the economy. For some countries these areas imply roles unique to government, but all governments will want to ensure that they receive due attention from the appropriate quarter. Central within them all is the need to "level the playing field" for those who – currently or potentially – are digitally and educationally excluded. Action to do this must be without stigma, which would itself lead to further exclusion.

The first objective is to **secure access for all to hardware and software**, since one of the major causes of the digital divide is the gulf between technology-rich and technology-poor homes, schools, communities and nations. The UK is setting up a national network of ICT-equipped learning centres, to ensure that those who cannot afford to buy their own computers, or cannot afford the telephone costs of Internet access, can nevertheless gain familiarity and expertise. Sweden and Finland are extending access to school premises out of normal hours. Several countries have schemes to recycle for education computers from commercial firms, that have been discarded in favour of more advanced equipment. In some cases such schemes extend to refurbishing the computers for use in the third world. A major policy concern to be addressed is the role of developed countries – the *haves* – in helping to bridge the digital divide for the rest of the world, the *have-nots*.

Provision of computer hardware and software is not enough. Government must invest in the **changed roles of teachers and learners**, to match the different priorities emerging in statutory education with the advent of ICT. Teachers need to be equipped to become confident and discriminating users of ICT, including familiarity with the World Wide Web, which implies the development and refinement of both technical and pedagogic skills. They need ongoing opportunities for professional development and exchange, becoming role models to their students as lifelong learners. The curriculum must adapt to value the development of skills and the ability to interact more than the retention of facts, a significant change which remains to be reflected in assessment and certification measures. Students leaving school must be confident and creative users of ICT and the Web.

Government has a major role in **promoting lifelong learning**, ensuring that all, especially those in danger of exclusion, have the chance to develop ICT skills and understanding. This involves creating positive images of learning, including learning with and about digital technologies, and encouraging people to understand and value the learning which they already undertake outside formal contexts. Most of those who resist learning do not see its relevance to their needs, and see no role models with whom to identify. Promotion is a complex and expensive issue, requiring different strategies for different groups, but is surely no less important than advertising the artefacts of the consumer society? The media have a role to play here.

Another role for government is in **quality assurance.** In a much more open market for education and training, more diverse opportunities will be offered by a greater range of providers. Individuals and organisations need information about the quality and benefits of what is available. In most countries, the state has traditionally controlled quality in education and training, but some of the methods used for this, such as regulating admission to courses, national curricula and qualification systems, may need to be reconsidered. New approaches are needed to understanding quality, new balances between process and content, competence and credentials. Governments may need to focus more on publishing information concerning the intellectual coherence and appropriateness of individual programmes and institutions.

The statutory period of schooling and the lifelong learning agenda are not simply about the vocational-skill needs of the global economy. New ways are opened up by ICT for **enhanced citizenship,** whereby people can participate in the governance of their communities and societies, through access to new knowledge, through the creation of debating forums which cross the boundaries of geography, time and social status. Governments are only beginning to understand that technological literacy can lead to greater political literacy and participation, a possibility which warrants active promotion.

For government, a sixth role is to develop **"brokering" services and agencies**. For instance, the biggest UK problem in the post-school education market is neither a shortage of suppliers (there are many) nor of demand (people respond when appropriate opportunities are made available). The real problem is the absence of intermediaries to help individuals to find their way through the maze of opportunities and providers, in order to match opportunity to need. Moreover, a broker is needed to identify unmet needs and provide feedback to the providers. The UK's *Learndirect* project has been designed with such a role in mind.

Government can **support, encourage and direct research**. We know surprisingly little about the impact of ICT on learning.[8] We know that the technologies offer great opportunities, and there is much visionary rhetoric. However, what is best learned through ICT and by whom? What are the optimum technologies for learning? We need new and more flexible approaches to research, since the rate of change means that our traditional approaches – with careful evaluation of pilot projects before wider adoption – are no longer feasible.

Finally, this report suggests that ICT and lifelong learning together imply a fundamental **change in the role of the policy-maker in education**. Change is too fast and unpredictable for conventional notions of planning, and the scale of educational need across the life-span for all citizens is too great for the public sector alone to meet. Governments need to act in partnership, helping to define objectives and develop strategies, in collaboration with other providers and with learners and potential learners. They will want to harness the resources of the private and voluntary sectors, of employers and trades unions, of communities and individuals.

---

8. The CERI project *ICT and the Quality of Learning* is itself addressing this issue.

CHAPTER 2
DIFFERENT EDUCATIONAL INEQUALITIES:
ICT AN OPTION TO CLOSE THE GAPS
by
Guillermo Kelley-Salinas[9]

DIFFERENT FORMS OF LEARNING GAPS

Recent years have seen extraordinary and accelerating developments in the pedagogical potential of ICT, to improve traditional school teaching and learning methods at all levels, and to offer greater diversity in the delivery of open and distance-learning programmes. Active participation in this process of continuous change is crucial for developing countries, but carries a double challenge. First, schools and universities must constantly adapt to the new technologies, such as satellite television, computers and information networks; since they can no longer perform effectively without these resources. Furthermore, society generates – and therefore demands for the professions and the workplace – a new technological culture, in which literacy and arithmetic skills are no longer enough.

However, the application of ICT in education may have important domestic and international repercussions in the context of existing inequalities. In less

---

9. Director General, Latin American Institute of Educational Communication (ILCE), Mexico.

developed countries, social inequalities are a fundamental problem, deeply rooted in demographic, economic and cultural factors. In order to provide the possibility of a more dynamic and fair social development, it is imperative for these countries to promote equity in educational opportunities. The equity issue must be addressed when ICT policies are adopted, lest existing inequalities are worsened by the digital divide. As in every large-scale process, there are inherent and important risks as well as great opportunities.

This chapter deals with the different origins and manifestations of learning gaps. The focus is on developing countries, though the gaps are also present in developed countries to some extent. Certain elements and strategies will be identified that are crucial to the design and implementation of ICT policies for improving coverage, quality and relevance of educational services. The Mexican Telesecundaria Programme will be described, to illustrate a successful innovation in bridging the gaps.

Socio-economic selection

Family income, rural or urban environments, the educational level of parents, nutrition and health are but some of the factors that condition access, levels of academic performance, and drop-out rates of children in school. It is these constraints, widely documented in the literature on educational inequality and reform, that are fundamentally responsible for school and social relationships being reproduced. According to UNESCO, literacy rates in "more developed regions" reach 98.7%, as opposed to 70.4% in "less developed ones", with a strong bias against women (UNESCO, 1998, p. 106). School enrolment is unacceptably low in less developed countries, except at the elementary level, which nevertheless exhibits high drop-out and failure rates. Public education systems tend to be rigid, with traditional and inadequate pedagogy, and only tentative use of ICT, so that they cannot respond to the diverse needs of potential learning populations.

The generation gap

The inter-generational gap is particularly severe in developing countries. Deficiencies often occur in the coverage, quality and diversification of the available learning opportunities, with an inadequate growth rate that may also be dysfunctional in relation to current needs. One of the most common shortcomings is in adult learning and workplace training, which lack rigour and are inadequately financed. Many adults lack the basic knowledge necessary for acquiring the skills and abilities demanded by the labour market, which forms one of the most significant obstacles to economic development. Furthermore, the minimal educational experience of parents has a negative influence on their children's academic performance, so the cycle of deprivation continues. It cannot be assumed that ICT will provide a ready solution to such problems, but in terms of access, costs and results, its efficient use may be the only way to satisfy the growing demand in adult and continuing education.

Regional gaps at the national level

Some of the most disturbing gaps can be seen by comparing the access to ICT and performance of isolated and disperse rural communities with those of urban areas. This problem is also present within the urban environment, as evidenced by differences in the quality of the education available to poor and middle-class neighbourhoods. These gaps are reflected in the number of the schools and their condition, as well as in the existence and level of complementary resources. In addition, teachers in rural areas usually experience difficult socio-economic conditions, and have fewer opportunities for professional development to acquire the needed new skills and abilities. The process of urban concentration and rural dispersion – which accelerates throughout the developing world – makes the problem of remote regions more acute and the use of distance technologies indispensable.

Academic performance inequalities within educational institutions

Cultural, ethnic and individual factors may also play an important role in determining inequalities within institutions and society. For example, inequalities that are gender-related or stem from individual learning styles are generally accentuated within rigid and conventional school systems, which reflect and reproduce the dominant social practices and prejudices. The appropriate use of ICT may have a significant impact here, because students with different learning abilities and backgrounds may follow individualised educational programmes that cater for their specific needs.

Compensatory programmes may be needed to prevent the perpetuation of inequalities for women and individuals who are especially challenged, more so in poorer societies. The African Girls' Education Initiative is a good example, involving 20 countries with specific programmes that allow girls to increase their participation in school and make available to them new information. Educated girls show new behaviours, such as marrying later, having fewer children, seeking medical attention sooner, and providing better care and nutrition for themselves and their children (UNICEF, 1999, p. 60).

Gaps at the international level

In most cases, the more developed nations have implemented high-quality educational systems with widespread coverage, accompanied by various additional services intended to address their most pressing social and economic needs. Despite their own rigidities and bureaucratic restraints, these systems have created curricular options that address the students' individual interests and meet the requirements of an ever-changing and demanding job market. In contrast, developing countries have been primarily concerned with achieving literacy and basic education for all children. They have not at the same time been able to reduce the growing gaps in quality and coverage of schooling at all levels.

The dynamics of the global economy and new trends in job diversification are set to widen these gaps, with universities in the rich nations at the forefront of scientific and technological research. Nowadays, high technology exports are just as important as manufacturing ones, and in some OECD countries, the creation and diffusion of knowledge generates almost half their gross domestic product (El Banco Mundial, 1999, p. 26). There is a synergy between their educational and economic systems, that less developed countries lack. This reinforces the existing international division of labour, and hinders the capacity of developing countries for a more coherent and equitable social development. These countries generally have a very well-educated elite, a small but growing middle class, and a large labour force that has not completed basic education, with hardly any middle-level technicians and professionals. The table below shows some relevant population and education statistics (UNESCO, 1998, pp. 106-110).

	Less-developed regions[*]	More-developed regions[*]
Population	5 000 million	885 million
Education expenditure, US $	248 billion	1 100 billion
Net secondary school enrolment	48.8%	105.8%
Higher education enrolment	8.8%	59.6%
Number of R&D scientists and engineers per million population	El Salvador 19	Japan 6 309
	Nigeria 15	United States 3 732

[*] As defined by UNESCO, 1998.

According to the World Bank (The World Bank, 1999, p. 235) "…in more developed countries the great majority of secondary schools and growing numbers of primary schools are now connected to the Internet. In some countries the majority of the schools became connected within a single year." Thus, Ireland in 1998 had 14% of its primary schools connected, but the proportion reached 95% in 1999. During the same period and at the secondary level, Portugal went from 30% to 100% school connectivity (OECD/CERI, 1999, p. 55). As far as the student-computer ratio is concerned, "some countries now average 2 or more computers per group of 30 children in primary schools; in secondary schools there are typically between 2 and 5 computers per 30 children". Between 1997 and 1998, for example, Ireland went from 37 to 18 students per computer at primary level, and Portugal from 65 to 35 at secondary. The United Sates has one computer to 8 primary students, while Sweden and Norway, who are leaders in this area, have one computer to 6 secondary students (*ibid.*, p. 53).

There are also great differences between the more-developed and the less-developed regions in the number of computers and Internet hosts per 10 000 inhabitants (The World Bank, 1999, p. 267):

	Less-developed regions	More-developed regions
Computers	120	2 690
Internet hosts	3	470

A GENERAL HYPOTHESIS

ICT brings to education the capacity to reach massive audiences with consistent quality of content, and to target groups with specialised needs. The use of the new technologies in developing countries could contribute to solving traditional learning gaps, reducing the educational lag of the adult population, and consolidating a national education system that offers quality services to all sectors of society. However, for this to occur to full potential, it is necessary to identify and comply with a series of conditions and strategies, based on the specific requirements and context of each country.

The impact and repercussions of ICT are two-fold. On the one hand, ICT may help significantly to increase delivery and coverage of educational services to the different segments of society, by offering more varied and flexible programmes, able to respond to an increasing and diversified demand. On the other, it may have considerable impact on the quality of education, in as much as it transforms the traditional teaching-learning process, to the point where a cognitive gap emerges between teachers and students with access to ICT and those without.

The positive effects on students of ICT in education include (Papert, 1997):

1   Enhanced motivation and creativity when confronted by the new learning environments.
2   A greater disposition to research and problem-solving focused on real social situations.
3   More comprehensive assimilation of knowledge in the interdisciplinary ICT environment.
4   Systematic encouragement of collaborative work between individuals and groups.
5   Ability to generate knowledge.
6   Capacity to cope with rapidly changing, complex and uncertain environments.
7   New skills and abilities fostered through technological literacy.

In general, all these effects raise the students' self-esteem and enable those who might be lagging behind their peers to become more self-assertive.

It is important to underline that ICT brings beneficial side effects in addition to the original objectives, with impact on the overall socio-economic context. These effects are seen in the creation of a new technological culture, with increased productivity and competitiveness in the economy and stimulation of lifelong learning. Moreover, the same technological infrastructure can be used for different educational objectives servicing other audiences. All such groups are then able to organise themselves to receive and use knowledge and information in new and unexpected ways. Such beneficial side effects, almost non-existent without ICT, are of particular importance to developing countries: the social returns are likely to be higher, with more people gaining benefit in more ways.

In sum, ICT can affect the pace at which the learning gap is bridged in developing countries, both domestically and in relation to other nations. The great challenge is to harness the advantages of those technologies, in order to improve the delivery and quality of educational services, as well as to accelerate the rate at which knowledge is distributed and learning chances and outcomes are equalised throughout society.

CONDITIONS AND STRATEGIES

Research and content development

Whether it be new learning environments, open and distance learning, teacher training initiatives, the incorporation of ICT into traditional school systems – these all require a sound policy of research and content development, as well as training of human resources in technical and pedagogical areas. For this, the participation of higher education institutions is critical, as is the analysis of international experiences, with the support and consulting services of multinational organisations. The construction of models that incorporate ICT is a complex task in several fields, particularly when directed to mitigating educational gaps. It involves formal curricular programmes, ranging from basic to higher education, and non-formal learning, from parent education to a variety of workplace training courses and continuous education programmes. There are also initiatives geared towards improving traditional services in general.

An important challenge is the design of effective models to integrate the content and processes of education with the technologies available for their delivery. It requires the participation of expert teachers and ICT specialists, to establish new methods of learning. Such liaison is also indispensable in the application to local needs and conditions of ICT knowledge from domestic or foreign research institutions. For this to function effectively, not only must these groups relate well to the educational bureaucracy, they must also be involved in pilot projects to test the different models.

Development of a flexible, open and cost-effective technological platform

It is essential to have a sound and adequate telecommunication and computer network infrastructure that can support and deliver diverse educational models. This infrastructure must be open and flexible enough to meet the country's needs, with appropriate procedures for its upgrading and maintenance. Account must be taken of the high level of investment required, in spite of the general tendency for prices to fall. It is therefore of the utmost importance to select the technological platform carefully, along with the right mix of economically viable software applications of suitable quality. Furthermore, the concept of technology as a magic key for solving all problems must not be the driving premise.

In many cases, the latest instructional models require state-of-the-art technology, but a more realistic and pragmatic strategy for developing countries may be a favourable combination of technologies, human resources, and infrastructure. The relative advantages of one technology over another may vary considerably, depending on the target audience and the learning model adopted. It may be appropriate to use simpler technologies such as radio for rural areas, and despite the fact that television as a learning tool has well known limitations, it still represents an economically viable and efficient option. This assertion, however, should not be seen as an argument for delaying the incorporation of on-line educational programmes. In fact, in some countries, educational television has encouraged the implementation of other initiatives in ICT, which today reinforce one another through a continuous process of technological convergence.

Unprecedented opportunities for knowledge dissemination arise in developing societies, through the exponential growth in ICT and the progressive reduction in cost. However, on-line tariffs and start-up costs are still very high, so that special rates may have to be negotiated for the education sector. The production of multimedia software could, with advantage, be de-coupled from the latest generations of increasingly sophisticated hardware specifications, which are well beyond the threshold of complexity and power needed for learning. This is true for both developed and developing countries.

Professional development of teachers

The use of new applications – text, video, CD-ROM, the World Wide Web or specific software – requires appropriate preparation for teachers, if the applications are to be effectively matched to content and learning objectives. It is imperative for sound in-service and pre-service teacher education and training programmes to accompany ICT initiatives for schools. Teachers must become comfortable with the technology and supported in the use of new applications, for instance with manuals and guides. A simple model of international collaboration between teachers from developing countries – *Teachers Talking About Learning* – was created by UNICEF.[10] Using the Internet and television, teachers exchange information, experience and advice on what works and what does not, and on how better to use the new technologies. An immediate benefit of this type of initiative is that teachers become confident users of ICT, and best practices are identified and disseminated.

A common myth is the idea that teachers in poor settings, and especially in rural areas, cannot make the great leap forward of assimilating and then using

---

10. See www.unicef.org/teachers/action/projects.htm

ICT. The MIT Media Lab Report *Project Lighthouse in Thailand: Guiding Pathways to Powerful Learning* discredits this belief (Cavallo, 1998). There had been strong reservations about the passive nature of Thai students, about the poor quality of instructors, particularly in poor and rural areas, and about capacity to change traditional teaching methods. Teachers were accustomed to lecturing without being questioned, and then testing rote knowledge; although they desired change, they were worried that it would need years of re-training, or new teachers. How could they adapt to technologically rich settings, with little education themselves and no experience in learner-centred classrooms? Many wondered whether they could understand the technology at all, let alone use it for teaching. The evidence, however, showed their fears to be unfounded. Thai teachers and learners adopted technologies fast and reliably enough to use them confidently and effectively.

The great advantage of ICT is not to substitute for teachers, but to enable teachers to enrich their teaching and their access to information. The new technologies also serve as an instrument for their own professional development. Teachers actively encouraged to generate new content and processes in their own language are thereby participating in the creation of global knowledge and have become indispensable for the educational process.

Parent education and compensatory programmes

When there are high levels of educational lag in the adult population, parent education programmes are perhaps one of the most important resources for reducing learning gaps throughout society. In the presence of socio-economic and family disparities, they provide a compensatory factor that lessens the negative influence of the children's environment. Due in part to the character of their audience, parent-education programmes may be easily adapted to distance formats, as is already done in several countries using radio and television.

Educational ICT is intrinsically compensatory in nature, due to the massive reach and homogenous quality that can be achieved. However, programmes directed to socially disadvantaged populations in developing countries need other compensatory measures alongside, such as school breakfasts, pre-school provision, salary incentives for rural teachers, health programmes and community-oriented initiatives. UNICEF has pointed out that cultures have long perfected ways of transmitting their accumulated knowledge and inherited wisdom to children (UNICEF, 1999, p. 22). But in a changing world, parents are not always able to put into practice all the new information that could be useful to them. Support has to be given to the parents, who are the children's first teachers.

Innovative approaches have been adopted in several countries, such as the "public kiosks" established in Turkey and Malaysia (The World Bank, 1999, p. 57). These kiosks, open to the general population, provide telephone, fax and even Internet connections. In addition to the obvious benefits, they allow direct communication between citizens and government agencies. For poor rural communities, Costa Rica and Malaysia are exploring the concept of *LINCOS* (Little Intelligent Communities), where tele-medicine, voice communication, access to the Internet, and many other services are provided (Figueres, 1999). The module is based in a low-cost, refurbished cargo container equipped with computers and communication links to low-orbit satellites. A trained community member takes charge of its operation.

Social participation

Social participation is essential for the successful development of ICT initiatives in education, the active involvement of the private sector and the local communities being critical. The community must be able to participate in and benefit from an innovation process of this nature, and additional resources for financing infrastructure and operation costs may be secured from the private sector. Given the commitment of entrepreneurs, unions, associations, local communities, and federal and state governments, technologies may be appropriately adopted and effectively utilised.

Much effort has to be expended in strategies that enable communities to take advantage of the new technologies, so that local populations become fully acquainted with their potential. For the specific purpose of encouraging and preparing teachers and community members, there are for instance *Community Mobilisers* in Brazil (Gropillo, 1999, pp. 10-11), *Telesecundaria Tutors* in Mexico (see below), and *Dinamizadores* in the Citizens' Participation Network of Colombia (Morales, 1997). These leaders raise community awareness of the potential of ICT, as a means of improving the quality of education and raising the standard of living in general. They are responsible for stimulating active community participation and commitment.

Planning and evaluation

In order to ensure effective and judicious incorporation of ICT, it is necessary to have coherent and comprehensive policies for planning and evaluation. These will include the definition of clear objectives, the identification of priorities and strategies, the ability to envisage future scenarios, the design, implementation and evaluation of pilot projects. Evaluation criteria and procedures must be determined in accordance with previously established goals and objectives, and field-testing should precede large-scale commitment. Planning must be rigorous but not inflexible, allowing refinement in the light of experience. When dealing specifically with learning gaps and exclusion factors, it is critical to start from a precise awareness of the nature and dimensions of these disadvantages.

Experiences from other countries are important, but their assimilation may require exchanges of information over a considerable time. International organisations such as the OECD's Centre for Educational Research and Innovation (CERI), and the Latin American Institute of Educational Communication (ILCE) can assist in the process of technology knowledge transfer. Countries helped in this way will be better able to assess their needs, to develop strategies and submit plans for financial support to multilateral lending agencies.

MEETING THE CONDITIONS FOR SUCCESS – THE MEXICAN TELESECUNDARIA

To illustrate how a successful distance-learning programme meets some of the criteria discussed above, a brief description of Mexico's television-assisted *Telesecundaria* programme is here presented. The middle-school programme has been in operation for 31 years, but the National Satellite Educational Television Network (EDUSAT) started in 1995, and now constitutes the means whereby Telesecundaria is delivered. EDUSAT has brought additional advantages, including the delivery via satellite of data, which makes it possible for communities and rural schools to join the Internet through *Red Escolar*, the Mexican School Net. Red Escolar offers – in Spanish – information for both teachers and students, in a wide variety of academic subjects; it fosters collaborative projects between schools, and provides in-service teacher training.

Telesecundaria was designed to meet the educational needs of hard-to-reach rural areas in Mexico, mostly communities of under 2 500 inhabitants. At first it was offered in a few states (there are 31 plus the national capital), with a little over 6 000 students. Today, the programme is available at 13 851 locations nation-wide, serves over 1 043 000 students and employs over 46 000 teachers (Secretaría de Educación Pública, 1999). The course comprises three essential elements:

- A 15-minute television programme, of which over 4 600 have been produced and up-graded over the years).

- Specially-prepared textbooks and teachers' guides.
- The teachers (tutors).

It is thus a mass system of formal schooling that combines distance programming with on-site teacher tutoring, and that offers two-way communication between the centre and the communities involved.

Children finishing the sixth grade in rural primary schools average lower academic performance than children from urban elementary schools. However, after the three-year Telesecundaria programme, the rural school students have caught up with their peers in traditional urban schools, suggesting a higher added-value for Telesecundaria learning. Telesecundaria has not only been successful in enhancing the academic performance of children in rural areas, but has encouraged their interest in staying at school through the entire cycle.

Unit operating costs per student are similar in the traditional system and the Telesecundaria schools, though it has to be said that average class size is slightly over 20 students for Telesecundaria and over 40 in regular schools (De Moura Castro *et al.*, 1999). Nevertheless, setting up and operating regular secondary schools in rural communities would cost nearly four times as much as normal. Furthermore, while overall enrolment in Mexican middle schools has grown at 3.3% per year over the last decade, Telesecundaria has registered close to 10% growth and it is expected to reach 12% next year, making in-roads into the semi-urban and urban sectors.

| | Student enrolment for the academic year | | Increase |
	1990/1991	1999/2000	
Telesecundaria	470 100	1 043 400	573 300
Total secundaria	4 190 190	5 264 097	1 073 907

During this decade, Telesecundaria was responsible for over 53% of the increase in student enrolment (Secretaría de Educación Pública, 1999).

A feature of the system is the cooperation between government and community. Usually the community provides a provisional venue while a permanent facility is built. In addition to sending trained tutors, the government makes available all necessary equipment and materials: parabolic dish, decoder, TV, VCR, desks, blackboard, textbooks, guides, notebooks, pencils, etc. The process becomes a remarkably rapid, flexible and efficient way to set up a school, without incurring high overheads. With a minimum of 15 students who have completed elementary level (K-6), a school can be started anywhere at the behest of parents or local authorities.

In Mexico where basic mandatory education includes the first nine grades, Telesecundaria appears to be the only way to serve a growing, scattered, and diverse potential population of middle school children. It works well because it:

- Follows a well-planned and researched academic model.
- Elicits and depends on community participation.
- Employs appropriate technologies in an effective and simple way.
- Provides extensive and continuous teacher training.
- Is constantly evaluated and up-graded.

In fact, it has proved so successful that other countries have implemented it at a national level. Thus far, Costa Rica, the Dominican Republic, El Salvador, Guatemala, Honduras, and Panama have between them over 20 000 students in their own versions of Telesecundaria. Furthermore, Bolivia and Colombia will begin pilot projects early next year and Ecuador has expressed its intentions to join (*ibid.*).

To be sure ,Telesecundaria has room for improvement. It is still in essence a vertical, face-to-face approach to schooling, if somewhat less overbearing. Work is needed to make it more interactive and more focused on the development of critical thinking skills, as well as on the solution of practical problems in the community. An issue yet to be addressed is that proportionally fewer Telesecundaria students have access to high school, compared with urban school children, which implies that inequality in social and economic status is still perpetuated. Even so, a measure of compensation has been achieved by the use of technology (satellite television) and other strategies, to reduce the learning gaps between rural and urban schooling, both in terms of access and quality of outcome.

Eventually, Telesecundaria will become Web-based. Actions are now underway to incorporate the Internet, and specifically Red Escolar, which was piloted in urban elementary and middle schools. This will give access via the computer to television, interactive video, Internet digital libraries and a myriad of on-line educational resources. It means that for the first time the Telesecundarias will be connected to the rest of the country's schools and able to participate in collaborative projects.

The Red Escolar innovation will have powerful effects not only for the Telesecundarias themselves, but also for their communities. EDUSAT and the

Telesecundaria sites constitute a platform from which knowledge and information can be distributed nation-wide for diverse purposes and to different audiences. In the Telesecundarias, community members gather outside regular school hours, to watch the Telesecundaria programmes from among the ten channels transmitted via EDUSAT. Thus farmers can take courses on crop raising, water management, or plague control; they can receive market information. Mothers are able to become better informed about general family health care and child rearing practices. Parents learn how to help their children study and in the process learn themselves. Youngsters receive seminars on issues such as AIDS and drug-addiction prevention. There is regular information on the services offered by the different federal and state agencies.

In the near future, Red Escolar will be widespread in Mexico's community centres, rural clinics, public libraries, elementary schools, and other local access centres. It will connect the urban and rural sectors and foster a culture of lifelong learning. Mexico is about to launch a Distance Secondary School for Adults,[11] for the development of basic competencies – reading, writing, arithmetic, the exercise of citizenship, the technological and scientific processes needed for practical-problem solving. Courses will be delivered via EDUSAT, and a Web page is in the making for those who have Internet access. Whilst this is a new programme, it has incorporated a substantial part of the Telesecundaria material. The intention of this learner-centred adult programme is to reach every site where there is a need for adult education at this level, including the workplace, schools, homes, community centres, hospitals and even prisons.

CONCLUSION

By itself education cannot solve the secular problems of social inequalities, but without equal access and quality learning for all, existing gaps will surely deepen. Educational reform has acquired a fresh impetus from the possibilities that ICT and the knowledge society bring to the cause of learning, equality and social transformation. New technologies constitute an extremely powerful tool to widen access and match the growing social demand for more diverse and pertinent education throughout life. The use of ICT is not an end in itself, however, nor is the objective simply to apply state-of-the-art technologies.

---

11. Secundaria a Distancia para Adultos.

Research is needed, including the evaluation of pilot projects, into how best to use ICT to meet curricular objectives, with the active participation of the academic community and society at large.

Developing countries must have a strategy for innovation. It is unlikely that they will be able to implement satellite and Internet educational systems at the same time or at the same rate. Where should they begin, and should they wait until costs come down appreciably? How will the high start-up costs be financed? They will need to establish teams of leaders with the required expertise. Teachers generally will require a thorough involvement and understanding, in order to apply the new technology and to create curriculum materials in their own language. Sometimes it will be necessary to implement sophisticated ICT measures even where there are no existing traditional educational programmes on which to build.

The developing world should move forward with alacrity to incorporate ICT in the learning process at all levels. Traditional applications such as radio and television lend themselves to diverse applications that are of great relevance, especially for rural populations, and will constitute an appropriate platform for achieving interactivity at a later stage, when the costs of two-way communication systems will become, in all probability, affordable enough. Even so, the use of computers and the Internet should not be delayed, so that within ten years all countries should be at approximately the same level of computer and Internet use.

The massive and multidirectional flux of information brought about by ICT has profound consequences on cultural and political settings, whereby the values of a pluralistic democratic society are reinforced, and the relationship between government and civil society becomes more transparent. Internationally, not only have the principles of tolerance and understanding been buttressed, but the possibilities for cooperation and exchange have multiplied. Against this scenario, regional inequalities in ICT come into sharp relief, and reinforce the case for assertive action towards closing the technology and learning gaps. This can be done in part through international collaborative projects, such as the OECD/CERI's *ICT and the Quality of Learning*, that disseminate information on successful practice and experience. Other international organisations will be able to encourage educational content production, in several formats and languages; they will be able to support the financing of relevant national schemes and foster the necessary technology transfer.

Different technologies are nowadays converging, so that the information networks – satellite, cable, fibre optics, telephone – will be used in complementary ways to deliver content in diverse formats to distinct educational audiences. The important thing is for the knowledge distribution between the poor and the rich to be more even. Investments then will flow more readily to the less developed regions of the world, where employment opportunities will increase at a faster pace. Educational opportunities made available through ICT might thus be a powerful means of overcoming social and world inequalities.

CHAPTER 3
THE DIGITAL DIVIDE: MAKING KNOWLEDGE AVAILABLE IN A GLOBAL CONTEXT

by
Nolan A. Bowie[12]

INTRODUCTION

The Internet is an instrument of communication that has great potential for positive change, in promoting free speech and other democratic principles. To many users the Internet is an empowering technology that enables individuals, communities and even nations to better their condition, that offers a strategic advantage in the knowledge-driven economy, and that opens new opportunity to enjoy a higher quality of life. Currently, those in the United States and around the world who are connected to the Internet – and who tend to be better educated and to have better jobs with higher incomes – are part of an elite class of *information-haves*: they go online to send and retrieve e-mail or to *surf* the Net for information, entertainment, shopping and other services.

---

12. Senior Fellow, John F. Kennedy School of Government, Harvard University.

In the networked society, economic well-being is knowledge-based (Stewart, 1997):

> • "Knowledge is more valuable and more powerful than natural resources, big factories, or fat bankrolls. In industry after industry, success comes to the companies that have the best information or wield it most effectively – not necessarily the companies with the most muscle. (p. x)
> • In this new era, wealth is the product of knowledge. Knowledge and information; not just scientific knowledge, but news, advice, entertainment, communication, service, have become the economy's primary raw materials and its most important products. (p. xi)
> • Knowledge has become the pre-eminent economic resource; more important than raw material; more important, often, than money. Considered as an economic output, information and knowledge are more important than automobiles, oil, steel, or any of the products of the Industrial Age. (p. 6)
> • If information is the greatest source of wealth, then individuals, companies, and nations should invest in the assets that produce and process knowledge. Those assets are not necessarily high-tech gizmos, and those investments should not all be high-tech investments." (p. 31)

Much of the drive towards "globalisation" comes from the increasing pace of change caused by the introduction of new technologies, that allow local businesses to enter into transactions with customers located anywhere. Those who have access to ICT *and* know how to use it effectively experience a host of beneficial possibilities, extending to the availability of resources such as tele-medicine and distance learning. However, there is increasing evidence of enormous variation in Internet access, both within and between nations and regions. Certain groups, communities, nations and regions of the world are effectively by-passed from the opportunities that the Internet affords. The *have-nots* generally consist of the poor, the illiterate, certain racial minorities, and the populations of the so-called developing nations – especially in Sub-Saharan Africa – where there is an inadequate infrastructure of higher education, electrification, and telephony (Melenga, 1999). This digital divide imposes new barriers on individuals, groups, communities and nations.

The Internet represents a potential force for positive change, but unless appropriate strategies are put in place, the new technologies might by-pass some communities and regions of the globe, thereby leaving huge populations of unconnected people beyond the margins of the information society. Although no one modality will serve for every situation, emerging wireless technologies may allow the *have-not* nations to avoid or postpone the more expensive telecommunications infrastructures based on twisted copper wire, coaxial cables and optical fibre. There is room and time for affirmative action on the part of governments, non-government organisations (NGOs), the market, corporations and communities, to mobilise public opinion and to ensure a just knowledge-driven economy and information society in which everyone has an opportunity to participate.

THE UNITED STATES – AHEAD OF MOST OF THE WORLD, BUT DIGITALLY DIVIDED

July 1999 saw the passing of a landmark in the United States, when for the first time more than 50% of United States households owned a personal computer – 53% compared with 39% in 1995, of which 37% have Internet access (*PC Magazine*, 16 November 1999). The figures say nothing about purpose, whether it is exclusively or primarily for game playing, word processing, "chatting" online with friends or interest groups, or more serious activities, nor about time and quality of use; they do not tell us why a majority of computer users has chosen not to go online. However, compared with most of the rest of the world, Americans are the information *haves*, although not the leaders in this respect – proportionally more in Finland and Singapore have personal computers and are connected to the Internet. Thus, for example:

> "Finland already has nearly universal access – it has more Internet hook-ups per person than anywhere on earth, twice the United States number, and will have every school in the country online by the year 2000. Electronic access is becoming an integral part of the democratic process in Finland, as much a guaranteed right as the right to vote."
>
> (Hammond, 1998, p. 60)

Between 1995 and 1999, the United States Department of Commerce produced three reports via its National Telecommunications and Information Administration (NTIA) unit, on the general theme *Falling Through the Net*. The first measured the extent to which households have access to telephones, computers, and the Internet. The second began to examine the digital divide, a process continued in the last of the three *Defining the Digital Divide* (NTIA, 1999). It was in these reports that the terms digital divide, *haves* and *have-nots* were introduced. Who are the *haves*?

"Those Americans enjoying the greatest connectivity today are typically high-income households. Holding income constant, other highly connected groups include Whites or Asians, middle-aged, highly-educated, employed (…) married couples with children, most often found in urban areas and the West. Conversely, the least connected generally [the *have-nots*] are low-income, Black, Hispanic, or Native American, senior in age, not employed, single-parent (especially female) households, those with little education, and those residing in central cities or especially rural areas." (NTIA, 1999)

Key findings within the 1999 NTIA report include:

*   Those with a college degree are more than eight times as likely to have a computer at home, and nearly sixteen times as likely to have home Internet access, as those with no more than an elementary school education.
*   A high-income household in an urban area is more than *twenty times* as likely as a rural, low-income household to have Internet access.
*   A child in a low-income White family *is three times* as likely to have Internet access as a child in a comparable black family, and *four times* as likely to have access as children in a comparable Hispanic household.
*   A wealthy household of Asian/Pacific Islander descent is nearly *thirteen times* as likely to own a computer as a poor black household, and nearly *thirty-four times* as likely to have Internet access.
*   A child in a dual-parent White household is nearly *twice as likely* to have Internet access as a child in a white single-parent household, while a child in a dual-parent Black family is almost *four times as likely* to have access as a child in a single-parent black household.
*   Whereas approximately 95% of White households have phones, the figure is 76% for rural-dwelling American Indians/Eskimos/Aleuts, and 85% for Hispanics and Blacks [but note that for the world as a whole, only about 50% of the population has ever made a telephone call, let alone owned a telephone *in their own home*].

THE GLOBAL DIGITAL DIVIDE – LITERACY, POVERTY AND ECONOMIC WELL-BEING

The world is not fair. The development in the West through the industrial age was not matched elsewhere. According to a study reported in Addis Ababa (Kendie, 1999), Africa has become increasingly marginalised in the world economy, as the following examples indicate:

- In 1955, the continent's share of world trade stood at 3.1%, but by 1992 the combined gross national product (GNP) of the countries of Sub-Saharan Africa was less than that of the Netherlands.
- Africa's debt burden, $13.1 *billion* in 1973, was by 1997 more than $315 billion, which exceeded the continent's total GNP.
- Africa has over 11 per cent of the world's population, but its share of world trade is small and has been declining, being in 1992 only 2% (and merely 0.9%, excluding the oil-exporting countries).
- Between 1980-1990, world trade grew at an annual rate of 6%, but the exports of Sub-Saharan Africa declined by 2.1%.

Although the focus of this chapter is access to information technology in relation to the digital divide, consideration of literacy is required here because of the nature of the rapidly changing, global, knowledge-based economy in which people must work, play and live. Even if everyone in the world could have a free personal computer, and free Internet access via reliable information infrastructures, that would not be enough. The technology could not empower those individuals who were illiterate and lacked know-how. Literacy itself is of strategic importance to individuals, regions and nations in the information society.

Whether or not real-time translations of the world's different languages will become realistically possible, the Internet today and in the near term is a text-based technology, where 80% of the global Web sites are written in the English language. So, at the very minimum, to achieve global Internet access requires literacy skills (notably in the English language) and the availability of a digital infrastructure. Let us then look at illiteracy as a significant contributor to the global digital divide.

A World Bank study on the quality of life (The World Bank, 1998), shows that some of the poorest *have-not* nations, with the highest levels of illiteracy, are also among those nations with the lowest life expectancy at birth. The table draws on these data and shows some of these countries, with 1995 figures for percentage adult illiteracy rates for males and females, aged 15 years old and older, and 1996 figures for life expectancy at birth.

Country	Adult illiteracy		Life expectancy at birth	
	Male	Female	Male	Female
Niger	79	93	44	49
Burkino Faso	71	91	45	47
Burundi	51	78	45	48
Guinea	50	78	46	47
Mali	62	77	48	52
Senegal	57	77	49	52
Sierra Leone	55	82	35	38
Togo	33	63	49	52
Uganda	26	50	43	43
Guinea-Bissau	32	58	42	45
Central African Republic	32	48	46	51
High income countries, average	**<5**	**<5**	**74**	**81**

The literacy gap (and therefore digital divide) between the poorest and the richest countries is apparent. Illiteracy must be addressed in the context of the fundamental issues of equity, poverty, human dignity, and quality of life of the *have-not* nations. Access to ICT and the availability of relevant information can help reduce historical inequities, by allowing quick response to crises and by providing the means to educate and inform, as well as serving as a means of transmitting medical assistance, diversions, news and entertainment – all while conserving energy and reducing waste and pollution.

Whilst illiteracy precludes taking full advantage of ICT, for many the most effective means to ensure literacy may be through the application of ICT. The issues of literacy (the key to knowledge acquisition) and access to ICT must be tackled together, including the telecommunication infrastructure. According to the International Telecommunication Union (ITU), the basic obstacle in the path of rapid Internet growth is the lack of telecommunication infrastructure. Although many countries have taken major steps to improve their infrastructure, great variation still remains between regions and countries. In Africa, over 30 countries still have less than one telephone line per 100 people compared with the global average of 13 per 100 (ITU, 1997).

Leapfrogging technologies and enabling strategies for closing the digital divide

How many are online? According to NUA Internet Surveys (NUA, 2000), the art of estimating how many are online is inexact, but their best estimate in June 2000 was a world total of 332.73 million, of which 147.48 million were in the United States and Canada, somewhat over a quarter in Europe (where there is considerable variation), and less than 1% in Africa.

Another survey (Strategis Group, 1999) suggests the present 44 million European Internet users may reach 170 million by 2003 (more than the United States), and that the 14 countries that account for 50% of the world economy will have 40% of their population online; China will then have nearly 34 million online, in a total worldwide of half a billion users. One key indicator of Internet access is the number of Internet host computers. At the start of 1998, there were about 129 300 host computers in Africa, of which all but 7 300 were in South Africa (Mannisto *et al.*, 1999). In Sub-Saharan Africa this was less than one per 100 000 people. The number of African Internet users averages about one per 5 000 people (excluding South Africa with one per 65), compared with a global figure of one per 45 people; or one per 6 people in Europe and North America.

According to the ITU (ITU, 1997), the lack of an extensive communication infrastructure might become an advantage for some African nations, in that when the telecommunication infrastructure is installed it will be digital from the start. Given that Internet services rely heavily on the degree to which networks are digital, developing nations might thus quickly reach the network conditions required for the provision of Internet services. For example, Botswana today has one of the world's most sophisticated national networks, and in countries such as Djibouti, Gambia, Mayotte, Mauritius and Rwanda, the main connections are 100% digital.

> "For the foreseeable future, the deployment of wireless networks is indeed the optimal solution to the information infrastructure gap in developing countries. Many developing nations have embarked on this road and a loose formula of employing fixed cellular networks for local loops [wireless]… and satellite transmission for long distance and international communications has emerged. [However] wireless networks deployed in developing countries have been decidedly voice-centric, with no provisions for the growing data and Internet communications having explicitly been made during the deployment of new networks."   (Kibati, 1999)

In theory, three geostationary communications satellites, with enough power and channels, could cover the whole world with a universal information and communications environment. However, instead of using only three communications satellites located in stationary orbits around 36 000 km in space, some companies plan to use between 250 and 700 Low Orbiting Satellites (LOS) at altitudes of 300-500 km, to relay telephone and e-mail messages and allow Internet connection. Not all wireless telecommunication, however, is based in space. Common earth-bound wireless technology includes television, radio, cellular telephone systems, paging devices, etc.

In 1996, Motorola launched the first of several novel satellite systems intended to extend cellular networks worldwide. It will feature hundreds of low-altitude satellites, allowing direct connection between cellular phones and hand-held computers, and hence communication between localities – including isolated villages – anywhere in the world. Other proposals include the use of stratospheric helium-filled balloons. Furthermore, a recent project *HALO* (High Altitude, Long Operation Aircraft) may provide a less-expensive alternative to satellites for metropolitan cities. In one such plan, one of three aircraft will fly for 8 hours in a 4 km circle at an altitude of 20 km over Los Angeles, followed in succession by the others, to supply multi-megabit bandwidth to a *footprint* 100 km across (Technology Front, 1999). Regardless of such schemes, the problem in developing nations remains one of making personal computers available, equipping the local population to use them effectively, and providing them with information – on agriculture, health, etc. – in appropriate languages and at low cost.

An excellent summary of significant technological trends in wireless telecommunications was prepared for the United States Department of Education (Hatfield, 1997). The trend is apparent – in both wired and wireless networks – of a shift from analogue to digital transmission (the Internet is digital). Noted also is that source coding is used in voice compression to remove redundancy from speech, so that fewer bits per second have to be transmitted to convey a voice signal, and the available bandwidth can be used more efficiently. Moreover, a provider can offer multiple services on a common network, or furnish the customer with end-user equipment able to receive different services from separate networks.

Power up

Concerns in the United States about the digital divide prompted the formation of a major multi-million dollar initiative, *PowerUp*,[13] involving more

---

13. November, 1999: see http://www.powerup.org.

than a dozen non-profit organisations, major corporations and federal agencies, including the Department of Education, to provide technology, funding and trained personal. The governing board consists of leaders from information technology industries, private foundations, former high-level government officials, and a top-level banking executive. These are people who have special insights, legitimacy and knowledge, regarding the marketplace, national security, and the enabling skills, experience, knowledge, infrastructure, and access requirements that will be needed for the knowledge-driven economy and society.

The *PowerUp* mission statement makes clear its views that access to technology and skills are vital to the economy and that quick but effective initiatives from both the public and private sectors are called for. Its purpose is to stimulate national awareness of the need to bridge the digital divide for the under-served young people in the United States, enabling them to acquire the skills, experiences and resources they need to succeed:

> "Access to technology and computer-based skills will be essential for children growing up in the new century and is vital to America's social and economic well being. The United States Department of Commerce estimates that by the year 2000, 60% of jobs will require skills with technology. And, the disparity between those with access to technology and those without will – if left unattended – establish an impenetrable barrier not only to quality jobs, but also to educational opportunities and access to information that all Americans will need in order to be successful. The United States can avert a potentially devastating new social inequality between digitally literate *haves* and *have-nots* if the nation's skills, resources and commitment are mobilised quickly."
>
> *PowerUp* Mission Statement

Even in the United States, there is recognition that to neglect the digital divide poses a danger to the entire economy and society; that it is in the nation's rational self-interest to begin to close any significant gaps and to begin preparing the nation's future workforce for the ever-emerging global, knowledge-based digital economy. Whilst no single organisation or solution exists for bridging the digital divide, it is nonetheless possible to identify a range of skills, experiences and resources necessary for the task, beyond the provision of hardware and software. These include innovatory curricula and assessment systems, adequate infrastructure and the professional development of teachers.

PowerUp brings together a powerful coalition of people and resources, designed to focus public attention on the potential crisis posed by the growing digital divide in the United States, and committed to building a better society. A national crusade will include putting technology, funding and other valuable resources into schools, community technology centres (CTCs) and other appropriate locations nationwide. This public-private initiative depends on the goodwill and efforts of concerned leaders from some of the industries that provide information services on the Net, but where they are unavailable, it is for the government to be the last-resort provider.

The elimination of the digital divide is seen to be of strategic national importance in the United States, which is the justification for government investment in communications resources and partnerships with the private sector. Other countries are making the same judgement, and may want to negotiate with multinational telephone and telecommunications companies, seeking their assistance in establishing first-rate institutions of higher learning, research and development, and in supplying the essential skills, experiences and resources that will enable their indigenous workforce to become competitive in the knowledge economy.

A crucial issue for any country is the extent to which there is an adequate and available information infrastructure, that allows all people the opportunity to access relevant information and communication technology, orally and via text now, and ultimately via multimedia (broadband services). The infrastructure may be the electronic networks of the Internet, telephone systems, or even broadband, high-speed cable television systems and cable modems. The system may use wire-based technologies, as with traditional voice-telephony, or electromagnetic radio and microwave frequencies for multimedia, or both. Wireless networks are often cited as the most economically feasible solution for developing countries in the first instance, since they avoid the cost of copper telephone lines and cable connections.

What are the new technologies?

There already exists a range of low-cost and affordable interfaces – hand-held digital devices, dedicated video-game consoles, Web-TV, smart-pagers, smart wireless-telephones, hand-held notebook computers, etc. – that provide access to e-mail or full Internet connectivity. Even so, without connection to the global network, these technologies are limited to game-playing or personal schedule making at best. Four examples follow:

- *WebTV* is a set-top box that allows Internet connectivity via conventional telephone lines. It is slow and lacks the high resolution of computer monitors. Currently the cost including keyboard is about $100, with monthly fees for access.

- *WinTV-D* is a low-cost ($300) receiver that enables PCs to receive digital and analogue TV, and high-speed data transmissions. It provides broadcasters and Internet-content providers with a single point-of-access to United States households, with sufficient bandwidth to simultaneously provide a nearly limitless number of consumers with a spectrum of services – television programming, digital downloads of software, music, movies, video games, and any other type of content.

- *Dedicated E-mail digital appliance/MailStation* is a compact device with a comfortable keyboard and a picture-driven menu, that lets anyone with a phone line have easy access to e-mail. It costs around $150, with a monthly charge for unlimited e-mail messages, regardless of source or destination (*Boston Globe*, 1999).

- *Dedicated game consoles with web browsing capability* (such as Genesis DreamCast or Sony II PlayStation) can offer relatively inexpensive Internet and e-mail access, when attached to an ordinary TV and phone lines, and may revolutionise the Internet (Fong, 1999).

Cisco Systems Inc. (Healey, 1999) is promoting wireless Internet connectivity, with technology that increases the range and the power of wireless signals and results in connections up to 380 times faster than the speediest dial-up modem (although speeds drop as more users share the network). The technology aims to solve one of the main problems for networks using wireless frequencies, that of reflected signals that interfere with transmissions. Those reflections force networks to cut back on the power of their signals, reducing their range and preventing them from penetrating foliage.

In 1999, some 225 million cellular telephones were sold worldwide, accounting for the sale of $10.7 billion worth of semiconductors. The market had already begun to shift toward data and Internet related features, including rudimentary types of Web surfing, in the expectation that by 2000 almost half of wireless phones sold would have built-in Web-browsing capabilities (Makoff, 1999). Motorola SA predicted that a billion people will be using cell phones by the year 2003, and, that a billion people will be accessing the Internet by 2005. Consistent with this view, cellphones enabled by Wireless Application Protocol (WAP) were introduced by Motorola, Nokia (Finland) and Ericsson (Sweden), to merge Internet communications with advanced telephony. People will have "the ability to access the same Internet content by voice, phone or computer – whichever is more convenient" (Crawford, 1999).

During the first week of November, 1999, the first known wireless Internet system over Multiple Multiplex Distribution System (MMDS) frequencies was unveiled in Africa by Communications Trends Limited (CTL). The so-called "Supernet 300" emphasised to a large audience in Lagos, Nigeria, the importance to Nigeria and Africa generally of the new technology, with its potential for enhancing education, culture and science. This microwave technology, comparable with cellular telephones, beats the problem of electromagnetic interference that is a hallmark of many analogue phone lines. Also, by using multi-user modems, some 20-60 subscribers can log on at the same time (Obasi, 1999).

Although as yet the sound quality of wireless communication falls short of traditional, wired quality, it appears likely that most voice telephone calls will someday be handled by wireless networks. Wireless operators must face the challenge of integrating European and American networks, which operate on different standards. There appears to be a shift away from the PC-dominated world towards a new focus on the Web as the way to connect people to business, ideas and entertainment. As consumers become more comfortable using the Internet to shop, gather information, entertain themselves and do business – and high-speed connections make those tasks easier – companies are anticipating that the e-commerce market could be as large as $1.5 trillion by 2003, when the worldwide Internet appliance market is expected to reach 93.7 million units, or $18.8 billion in sales, from 13.8 million units, or about $4.6 billion, in 1999.[14]

CONCLUSION

John Chambers (Chambers, 1999) argued that we shall see educational use of the Internet exceeding e-mail in scale, since it can provide faster learning at

14. Source IDC: see http://www.idc.com.

lower costs with more accountability. He sees companies driven to keep improving productivity, in an intensely competitive global economy, with their survival dependent on their ability to relate to one another through the Internet. Whereas participation in the industrial revolution required being in the right country or location, capital in the future will flow to those countries and companies that install the best Internet and educational capabilities. The full effect of this, which may yet take about ten years, will affect the global balance of economic power. Kaku (1997) sees a future in which the Internet is everywhere:

> "In the third phase of computing, invisible computers will converse with each other, eventually creating a vibrant electronic membrane girding the earth's surface (…). From now to 2020, computer scientists expect to see an entire world blossoming over the Internet: electronic commerce and banking, cyber malls, virtual universities and schools, cyber libraries, and so on (…).
>
> By 2020, microprocessors will likely be as cheap and plentiful as scrap paper (…) allowing us to place intelligent systems everywhere. This will change everything around us, including the nature of commerce, the wealth of nations and the way we communicate, work, play and live.
>
> This steady exponential explosion in computer power, in turn, will spawn entire industries that have no counterpart in today's market. When the price of a computer chip is just one penny, the financial incentive to include them everywhere, from our appliances to our furniture, our cars, and our factories, will be enormous. *In fact, companies that don't include a few computer chips in their products will be at a severe competitive disadvantage.*"

On 21 November 1999, President Bill Clinton spoke at an informal *Third Way* conference in Florence, Italy, at which five other world leaders also participated, concerned with spreading the benefits of technology equitably (Hunt, 1999). He suggested the goal of access to the Internet on the same scale as telephone usage within a fixed number of years. Developed countries should work towards getting the technology to poorer nations. Both the President and the British Prime Minister, Tony Blair, saw the need for more money to be spent on education, since the economy today is knowledge-based. The opportunities and risks for the world population remain as they had been described some four years earlier (Lavin, 1995):

> "Less advanced countries that cannot upgrade their infrastructures and practices to the levels required by a global information economy will remain trapped in the traditional dilemma of *commodity economies*. More of their energy will be spent exporting natural resources (including labour) at depreciating prices and servicing their external debts. Little or no resources will be left for any longer-term social or economic investment. Their national economies will not be able to escape the vicious circle of poverty, and a large share of the world's population will remain at the periphery of the global information economy. Understandably, these countries would then be tempted to regard the global information economy as a new instrument of exploitation of the poor by the rich. Hostile North-South rhetoric would flare anew, as it did in the 1970s with discussions of a new world information order and a new international economic order, and opportunities for mutual benefits would be lost. Tension would become endemic between the *telecommunications rich* and the *telecommunications poor* (the *haves* and *have-nots* of the global information economy), further jeopardising the promise of joint wealth creation offered by the global information economy."

CHAPTER 4
Emerging Trends and Issues: The Nature of the Digital Divide in Learning

Synthesis by the OECD Secretariat

INTRODUCTION

Ample illustrations of the digital divide in learning were put forward during the Roundtable. Such illustrations show that there is no single, clearly-defined divide, but rather a series of gaps, brought about by a variety of factors which often come together, many of which do not have their roots in the technology itself. There are those, however, who take exception to the term digital divide, seeing it as negative and unhelpful, and fearing that such emphasis will undermine the potential of ICT to open new horizons in accessing knowledge and information; the hope appears to be that enthusiastic affirmation of the benefits of ICT will be enough to ensure its widespread adoption. Others again see the term digital divide as coined to create alarmism about a supposed ICT skills shortage, a marketing ploy to boost the sector.

Such scepticism about the notion of the digital divide was not the view of the Roundtable, as participants acknowledged the complexity of the related issues and their interpretation. However, given the existence of manifold "divides", how real is the risk that the term digital divide is a loose attention-seeking expression of limited practical value? Questions were raised about the distinctiveness of the *digital* aspects of learning inequalities, as opposed to other more familiar and perennial social aspects. Should learning's digital divide be regarded as a critical new problem, or as but the latest manifestation of longstanding familiar problems – and no less important for that? Does it show elements of both these positions? Acknowledging the existence of the digital divide does not imply that the causes are themselves merely technological, as the following Roundtable quotation indicates:

> "With the remarkable advancements in information and communication technology (ICT), there is now a genuine concern about the *digital divide*, the gap between the ICT *haves* and the ICT *have-nots*. There is a good justification for this concern and the figures show it at every level. But narrowing the divide – publishing a newspaper in every village, placing a radio and TV in every household, putting a computer in every classroom, and wiring every building to the Internet – does not automatically solve the problem. The most serious divide is in the *extent and quality of human knowledge and learning*. It is not digital, it is educational."
>
> *Wadi D. Haddad*

This chapter presents insights from the Roundtable discussions and submissions on the diverse dimensions of the digital divide, as an addition to the main contributions presented in the previous two chapters. It points to a more thorough analytical understanding, but given the nature of this source material, it makes no pretence to offer comprehensive coverage. What can best be done in response to the digital divide through different policy strategies and programmes forms the focus of the next section of this report.

LEARNING AND THE DIGITAL DIVIDE – DIMENSIONS AND ISSUES

As expressed by a participant, the digital divide in learning and education is in fact "a whole landscape of problems". One typology offered to gain a better grasp of this landscape looks at the patterns (and problems) of ICT access and use for education and learning, in relation to the following sections of the population:

- Those with special needs or physical disability
- The socially and economically deprived
- Linguistic and ethnic minorities
- Groups suffering social exclusion
- The geographically remote
- Older citizens, for whom new technology has arrived late in life
- The technologically-alienated or apathetic   *Robin Ritzema, U.K. Representative*

Other categories emerged during the Roundtable discussion, not all of which relate to particular population groups. Some refer to gaps between educational settings and others to whole countries and regions, a range that is reflected in the points which follow.

Formal education – Gaps in investment levels

Perhaps the most obvious manifestations of the learning digital divide are the ICT gaps that exist *within formal education*, between one school or school district and another, in terms of the equipment, materials, connectivity, professional competence, and integration of ICT within the teaching/learning environment. Many participants suggested that these represent only the most basic indicators – the actual educational use of ICT and changes in student competence being more fundamental – but major differences are apparent. Whilst the OECD 1999 summary analysis (see below) and many national surveys seek to chart these aspects, hard data are insufficiently available and much depends on anecdotal evidence only. It will be important to develop convincing frameworks for the gathering of data and analysis of the educational digital divide.

"The figures [students per computer] show wide variations at both levels, but the greatest range in primary. Where figures over two years are available, the rise in computer intensity is marked; at the extreme, Ireland has halved the number of students per computer in a single year. The most ICT-intensive countries in education are the United States, Finland, New Zealand and Sweden. They have 7 pupils or fewer per computer in secondary education and 13 in primary education. The United Kingdom, Denmark, Ireland and Norway have good access to ICT (…) The age and quality of computers in schools is crucial: only if they have sound cards and CD-ROM drives, for example, can students use up-to-date and efficient multimedia software including access to the Internet. Data on the proportion that have this multimedia capacity are only available in some countries, but show that despite rapid progress, a large number are out of date in this sense." (OECD, 1999)

Evidently some of the key inequalities in educational ICT investment are associated with differences between countries, levels of education, quality of ICT equipment (and the educational uses it permits), and Internet connectivity. However, as the OECD extract also mentions, there are problems of gathering a meaningful picture of developments when the pace of change quickly outdates the available summary statistics.

There is an important role for schools and other educational institutions to ensure equality of access to ICT, and thereby to raise *technological literacy* throughout the student population – a basic learning aim. It has to be noted that many aspects of the digital divide are determined by ICT access and use outside the formal system, but as a number of participants recognised, schools and other educational institutions can play a compensatory equalising role. There are aspects of the divide which are profoundly social rather than technological.

There was lively exchange on the potential for distance learning to overcome forms of cultural or social separation, other than the barrier of geographical distance. Some maintained that this represents a very promising way in which ICT can help to address various social divides in learning, others that distance learning is just as prone to unequal access and participation as the more conventional programmes. Reference to tertiary education arose in the context of lifelong learning, though there was little Roundtable discussion of the digital divide as found in this phase of education, and few data are known to exist. Nonetheless, there is no reason why access to ICT and its use in learning should be any less relevant in the higher reaches of the formal education system than for schools.

ICT use – Learners and teachers

It is important to gain a more robust understanding of gaps in educational ICT investment. Several participants stressed, however, that the simple indicators of equipment levels commonly used may be quite misleading. What matters, it was suggested, is the actual *use* made of ICT. A related caution concerned the need to distinguish between accessing information and engaging in constructive learning, the goal being the latter and not simply the former. Learning through ICT is evidently not possible in the absence of such things as computers, CD-ROMs, e-mail and connectivity, but whereas these form the *necessary* conditions, they are not themselves *sufficient*.

The relevant questions concern not just whether ICT is regularly used in educational settings, but how it is used. For instance, New Zealand research reported at the Roundtable suggested differences in how ICT is adopted by teachers and students: high socio-economic status schools tend to use it for advanced applications and thinking, whereas other schools are more likely to focus their application on basic-skill development, or – worse still – on diversionary activities such as computer games. It seems that the different approaches to learning adopted by different types of school are explicable in terms of the social intake of the student population. One Roundtable participant described how the exemplary use of ICT by students for multi-disciplinary research and problem-solving is essentially an inductive process. As such it may run sharply up against the deductive and rule-driven assumptions of many education systems and schools.

Much more evidence could be compiled from different countries and types of schools, on the nature and social distribution of the use of ICT in education. How far do privileged educational institutions use ICT to reinforce their advantages? Alternatively, have actual cases been charted where the imaginative educational use of ICT has helped to overcome a range of outstanding problems in order to bridge divides? It is to be expected that evidence could be found in support of both positions, suggesting that while educational inequalities may often be compounded by ICT, it can act as a liberating force. Given wide differences in use and application, the interpretation of evidence will need great care.

The existence of divides in ICT use leads immediately to issues about teachers – their preparedness for the integration of the new technologies in the classroom, and the extent to which they actually do so. It will be important to gain a clearer picture of these factors. Which teachers in which schools already use ICT on a regular basis, and for what tasks? Which teachers never do? How does the picture vary according to level and type of education – primary or secondary, public or private? What is the effect of the age and gender of the teacher, of subject specialism, of country? What sort of professional development have teachers been involved in, and how closely does this professional development shape subsequent applications in the classroom? On all these questions, there is a dearth of reliable information.

As evidence becomes available it will need to be understood in context. In those schools and systems where the classroom deployment of ICT is encouraged, differences in actual practice may closely reflect teacher characteristics. In other cases, it may be misleading to assume that the lack of exploitation of ICT is principally to do with teachers' own capacities and interests, being perhaps a consequence of other constraints within the system. A further question raised during the Roundtable discussion is whether there is any evidence of significant gaps opening up between teacher and student, in relation to the cognitive processes of ICT use, with students (but not teachers) characterised as belonging to the "Nintendo generation". Are such generation differences more difficult to traverse than those of earlier times, or are they simply their latest manifestation? These questions remain open for the present.

ICT skills – Different population groups

Thus far in this chapter, the gaps described in relation to the digital divide have been outlined in terms of *inputs* (investments in hardware, software, and teacher preparedness) and *processes* (ICT use in schools and classrooms). The obvious further dimension to be charted concerns *outcomes* – the differences across many different groups in society in terms of ICT skills, confidence and competence acquired. Whilst the necessary investments must first be in place, it then becomes vitally important to empower people to make use of them, as another Roundtable quotation indicates:

> It is necessary but not sufficient to provide avenues to information and knowledge. What is more important is to **empower people with appropriate educational, cognitive and behavioural skills and tools** to:
> - access the information avenues efficiently, effectively and wisely;
> - acquire knowledge and internalise it;
> - apply knowledge to better understand the changing world, to develop their capabilities, to live and work in dignity, to participate in development, to improve the quality of their lives, and to make informed decisions; and
> - upgrade their knowledge continuously and systematically.
>
> *Wadi D. Haddad*

Other skills and competence could no doubt be put forward to define literacy, to incorporate the important technological dimension in today's world. Whatever the precise specification, however, the point here is that when attention focuses on outcomes, it gives an added dimension to the digital divide. Once the shift is made from inputs and processes to outcomes, then the factors that go to explain inter-group differences come into focus, not all being within the education system itself. The view was expressed during the Roundtable that much research interest is directed at the technology, but little at the attitudes, values and experiences of the user groups, their material circumstances and prospects.

Gender is clearly one important dimension in relation to the digital divide, along with the interactions between gender and other social and cultural variables, such as poverty and ethnicity. Women in many societies are much less likely overall than men to have effective access to ICT, but men also may be severely disadvantaged. The Roundtable heard that in New Zealand, adult males in their 40s and 50s with insufficient skills and poor qualifications form just such a group, among whom disadvantages have accumulated and become acute.

In the New Zealand example, the technology learning gaps might equally have been described as *inter-generational*. The problems encountered by older workers left behind by technological change are familiar, as are issues relating to the semi-retired and the retired. Such issues are only partly defined by the difficulties of labour market marginalisation. For the elderly a range of other factors – personal, health, community involvement – may be of still greater importance, as ICT is coming to play a pervasive and critical role in society. There are indications that familiarity with and use of ICT is greater among the retired population than might have been expected, but as with other groups the interaction of various dimensions – gender, income level. education, ethnicity – needs to be carefully disentangled.

Ethnicity and cultural communities represent an essential focus for further analysis of the digital divide. Such communities, possessing their own specific characteristics, are found across OECD and non-OECD countries. It cannot be assumed that they share any common experience relating to ICT use and learning. Sometimes ethnic groups will display the familiar patterns of educational disadvantage, reinforced by social and economic problems. In other cases advantages are in evidence. One participant referred to Mexican parents and students in the United States, for whom home use of computer and Internet has led to positive effects on learning and enhanced motivation. It would be useful to compile similar examples from ethnic and cultural minority communities in other countries. One Roundtable conclusion from such examples was the need to recognise the importance of informal learning, in negotiating the different contours of the digital divide. This is the focus of the next section.

Gaps in informal learning – Homes, workplaces and communities

Educational policies that aim to bridge the digital divide risk leaving untouched some of the most influential aspects – notably the *home differences* in computer and Internet access that are charted elsewhere in this volume. Different viewpoints and scenarios were suggested relating to home/school relationships. At one extreme most student home-computer use was seen as devoted to game-playing, though even here it might be argued that a range of technology skills is being honed, perhaps for profitable application later. A contrasting view was that many relatively privileged students are already active in out-of-school electronic networks, thereby furthering their own education and hence their advantage. The latter view clearly implies much greater concern about the need to bridge home-related inequalities.

A further contrast was offered in terms of broad scenarios put forward as possible futures. In one, the school is portrayed as being in terminal decline compared with the home and home learning. On this scenario, home-based ICT differences will become more fundamental determinants of the digital divide. The contrasting scenario has schools maintaining and indeed enhancing their relative community importance, but this was seen as contingent on greater levels of educational investment than many countries have yet been willing to afford.

There are broader *non-formal learning* digital divides than those defined in terms of individual households. Some work and community settings can be described as "technology-rich", others as "technology-poor". important divides exist between well-resourced and poor communities, even when they are in close proximity, a striking example being the so-called *Silicon Valley* in California. Another related example mentioned by several participants is the gap that can exist between urban and rural communities, though this is a gap that has forced into existence some of the most innovative examples of ICT use for distance learning.

The workplace deserves particular attention as an important locus for the reinforcement of many inequalities. Certain professional settings and career routes bring with them exposure to advanced technology in the routines of working life, while others are simply "technology poor". Thus advantages may be accumulated or barriers compounded. Exposure to and use of professionally relevant technology develops competences that serve to open further doors in the job market, while other work settings offer scant access to transferable technology skills. Even when education policies have succeeded in giving individuals a solid basis in ICT competence, such individuals risk losing that foundation in non-technological environments – the "use it or lose it" principle.

The Roundtable heard of the Office of Learning Technologies (OLT), set up by Human Resources Development Canada,[15] to contribute to the development of a lifelong learning culture and expand innovative learning opportunities through technologies. OLT distinguishes between the more formal technology learning that is organised through training and that which occurs as part of working and the normal functioning of an enterprise. It confirms the problematic status of small firms regarding skills development, and is interested in the hierarchical inequities between management and other levels of the workforce in their technology learning. Studies of this kind are an essential aspect of building up an information base on the digital divides of learning in diverse non-formal settings. The significance of informal learning was emphasised by a Roundtable participant:

> "(…) most learning happens outside educational institutions, and well away from the control of teachers. Recent research by Eraut in the UK has confirmed that most of the most important learning which industrial workers undertake happens in and around the workplace, not on training courses or under formal supervision. Notions of 'instruction' and 'classroom' are simply irrelevant, and we need to think much more radically. I would argue that 'curriculum' continues to exist, but it has at its core not how learning processes are organised by teachers in classrooms, but how the processes of the workplace and the community are organised to make learning natural and inevitable."
>
> *Stephen McNair*

National and international disparities

There are the very wide *national disparities*, between the richest countries of the world (notably the United States to which most of the existing data relate), and other countries with much lower or minimal technology use in education, homes, enterprises and communities. The OECD *Information Technology Outlook* (OECD, 2000, p. 36), for instance, provides data up to 1997 that permit the gaps to be measured in terms of expenditure on ICT as a percentage of gross domestic product. Whilst the percentage stands at nearly 9% in New Zealand, and is relatively high in Sweden, Australia, the United States, Switzerland, the

---

15. See http://olt-bta.hrdc-drhc.gc.ca.

United Kingdom, Canada and Japan, it falls to less than 4% in Mexico, Poland, and Turkey. As with other manifestations of the digital divide, the tendency appears to be that the most privileged are able to enhance their advantage.

ICT developments have been an integral part of the globalisation process, as major time and location constraints have been removed in the processing and communication of data and the exchange of services. In consequence there is an international dimension to the digital divide, including a gulf between North and South, which leaves poorer countries disadvantaged. However, as with other manifestations of a divide, ICT which exacerbates inequalities may yet be the very vehicle for redressing them. One participant expressed it thus:

> "The new worldwide economy produced by economic developments and advances in ICT is (…) high speed, knowledge driven (…) competitive. Countries have to meet the competitiveness challenge (…) The good news is that, with the potential of human development and advanced technologies, developing countries can leapfrog. The bad news is that this process is not automatic. On the contrary, unless conscious efforts are made, countries are likely to be marginalised."
>
> *Wadi D. Haddad*

Apart from concern with economic issues, worries were expressed during the Roundtable about the homogenising impact of globalisation and the risk this poses to cultural diversity. A repeatedly-expressed concern related to *linguistic gaps*, given the software and Internet dominance of the English language. Such concerns do provide tangible targets for policy, however, as shown by the Portuguese example (see Chapter 9).

Issues arising

From examination of these different dimensions, the basic question remains as to whether or not learning has a digital divide. On one side, it can be maintained that ICT simply gives another expression to the profound, longstanding divisions of social class, ethnicity, gender and geography. On the other, ICT is seen to be of such importance to society and the economy, that low technological literacy has come to represent one of the most important forms of exclusion. A synthesis of both viewpoints is needed.

First, there is clearly a need to understand how the digital divide is manifested among different groups and communities, rather than regard it as a specifically "technological" issue. There is a need to understand the ways in which ICT can exacerbate or alleviate a variety of existing inequalities. Technological competence has become a fundamental aspect of literacy and citizenship in the 21st century, making its lack a determining factor of exclusion. Those with little or no ICT competence are denied access to powerful new forms of learning and information sources, a double exclusion. The more deeply immersed we are in the technology, the more we take it for granted, making the divide still greater for those who are excluded. It follows that, without careful analysis, many aspects of this divide will remain undetected, including those relating to private computer and Internet use. The significance of the digital divide *per se* should not be under-estimated.

It was observed that, when the technology does not work well, it can be especially de-motivating for those with least. This is either to argue for high levels of technical support for non-traditional learners, or to warn against over-reliance on ICT for tackling the learning problems of the disadvantaged. A number of interventions supported the point articulated in Chapter 2, that many technologies other than the most "cutting edge" should be deployed in expanding access to learning, including both radio and television.

A dynamic perspective is needed to address the dimensions of the digital divide, which was referred to as a moving target, where new problems come into view as others are resolved. Profound issues of philosophy and approach are raised. One speaker asked whether ICT will contribute to widespread new approaches to learning that are less bureaucratic and less homogeneous. Another called for schooling to give much greater attention to knowledge *creation* rather than knowledge *transmission*: the new technologies can make a fundamental difference to the quality of learning when they are integral to the former rather than simply vehicles for the latter. For other speakers, the very possibility of ICT to promote equitable opportunities is an element of its democratic appeal. Profound issues are clearly at stake.

There is growing interest in the power of ICT to provide a medium for cultural exchange, within which diversity is promoted. The G8 meeting (the eight major industrialised democracies) in Okinawa, July 2000[16] agreed to

---

16. See http://www.g8kyushu-okinawa.go.jp.

establish a *Dot (Digital Opportunites Task) Force*, to find how international cooperation might help to bridge the digital divide. Among the tasks to be undertaken was giving positive encouragement to the use of ICT with indigenous language. The promotion and celebration of cultural diversity is itself seen to be a motivator in the use of ICT for economic development, so that *digital diversity* becomes a way of bridging an aspect of the digital divide:

> The dot force will find ways for "(…) encouraging the production of locally relevant and informative content including the development of the content in various mother tongues."
>
> Okinawa Charter on Global Information Society, para. 19

> "Experience shows that diversity can arouse interest, engender initiative and be a positive factor in communities seeking to improve their economies, particularly when assisted by the extraordinary means of the IT society. We shall strive to promote the digitalisation of cultural heritage (…)"
>
> G8 Communiqué Okinawa 2000, para. 41

It might indeed be maintained that of all the different manifestations of the digital divide – in commerce, the media, public administration and the like – perhaps the most important concerns education and learning. The fundamental role of ICT in contemporary life is in relation to knowledge, competence and expertise, which is not at all the same as identifying the key variables to be narrowly *technological*. ICT is a *means* and not an *end*:

> "I suspect the real access issue is going to be a different kind of access – as the price of technology declines, the problem will not be access to hardware and software, but access to the knowledge needed to know how to use it – to make technology used and useful."
>
> *Robert D. Muller, U.S. Department of Education*

CHAPTER 5
The Digital Divide Within Formal
School Education: Causes and Consequences

by
Richard L. Venezky[17]

INTRODUCTION

Although schools in most industrialised countries have taken strong measures to ensure equal access to ICT resources, inequalities continue to exist. To understand what measures might be effective for eliminating these remaining differences, it is necessary to partition the problem into at least three classes. In the first, here called the *missing link*, are students with specific disabilities and those in schools in remote rural or poor inner-urban areas where telecommunications are limited and expensive. For these groups, technological and economic solutions are required for access. For the second class, however, here called the *wasteland*, the very nature of ICT is the problem that needs to be corrected. This class is occupied by women and girls and by some minorities, who find computing too solitary, isolating, and mechanical. To attract females to ICT, software needs to be redesigned to appeal to a wider audience, the image of the computing world needs to be softened and made less antisocial, and

---

17. OECD and University of Delaware, United States.

computer games need to be made more imaginative and less violent and redundant. Similar considerations need to be made for other sub-populations who so far have shunned ICT.

The third class, the *foreign language*, is composed of students typically but not exclusively from high poverty homes and other places on the periphery of society. These students need guidance to take advantage of the new opportunities and resources that ICT provides. The digital divide for these students is not simply an equipment differential that can be overcome with further selective investments in hardware, software, and networking. Instead, the inequalities of concern derive from both within school and within home differences that influence academic aspirations and capacity for self-directed learning. Student self-learning ability is a critical factor that allows some students to profit more than other students from such open ended resources as ICT. National policies directed toward closing the digital divide for schooling must attend to all of these contributing factors to be successful.

THE NATURE OF THE DIVIDE

Several chapters in this volume have delineated characteristics of the digital divide; however, it is instructive to probe these data for a more precise description of what is unequally distributed and why we should care about it. After all, society is full of inequalities that are widely tolerated without excessive pangs of discomfort or guilt. Some countries have lots of natural resources and others do not; city dwellers usually have access to lots of movie houses and rural dwellers do not; people with high incomes or high personal wealth have access to the best health care. Furthermore, schools in more affluent areas have for decades had more computers than schools in less affluent areas, yet no national or international concern has resulted.

The digital divide is not exactly about computers *per se* but about access to the world of information and communication. At the core of the digital divide are the newer information technologies – e-mail, the World Wide Web, and file transfer protocols in particular. Not everyone restricts the digital divide to these resources, however. A recent report from the American Association of University Women, *Tech-Savvy: Educating Girls in the New Computer Age,* chose the terms "computers" and "computer technology" as proxies for the "larger 'e-culture' of information and simulation" (AAUW, 2000, p. i). A report from the Disability Statistics Center at the University of California-San Francisco mentions computer ownership and Internet use in relation to the digital divide among disabled people (Greene, 2000). In contrast, a study by the College Board in the United States, *The Virtual University and Educational Opportunity,* is primarily concerned with virtual courses taught over the World Wide Web (Gladieux and Swail, 1999).

In spite of these variations, the World Wide Web is the sine qua non of the digital divide. If it did not exist, it is unlikely that such concern would be raised over the unequal distribution of computers by gender, race/ethnicity, urbanicity, or any other factor. Computers by themselves (*i.e.*, as stand-alone devices) are powerful assistants for word processing, numerical analysis, data management, and the like; they are also useful for entertainment and for some types of instruction. They appear, according to some but not all analyses, to raise productivity in industry (see Triplett, 1998 and Gibbs, 1997 for reviews). However, no data are available on how home computers affect personal productivity. In general, keeping one's family tree on a computer, especially with the assistance of a genealogy programme, can be more efficient than keeping the same records on paper. However, recipe files on-line are a less certain advantage. Given the high percentage of jobs that now require or involve computer use, some concern should and does occur over the capacity of schools in high poverty areas to teach computer skills. It is doubtful, nevertheless, that a major digital divide would have been declared if competence with stand-alone computers were the only issue.

A similar argument could be made about the Internet without the World Wide Web. Technically, the Internet is a series of physical interconnections and information transfer protocols that allow a variety of applications, including e-mail and the World Wide Web to operate. Expressed differently, the World Wide Web and e-mail ride on the back of the Internet, just as a national mail system might ride on the back of rail and air systems that exist independently. If e-mail and a few other Internet based facilities (*e.g.*, file transfer protocol) were available, but without the World Wide Web, it is doubtful that the President of the United States and the Prime Minister of the United Kingdom would each have addressed a digital divide in major speeches, as they did in the past year. What has enabled the information revolution as well as the virtual university is the World Wide Web, and convenient access to it grows more and more essential every day. So far, full access to the World Wide Web requires a computer. Some pagers and wireless phones will display text from the Internet or WWW – stock quotes, e-mail messages, etc. – but hypertext, colour graphics, forms that can be filled and out and submitted, and animation require a colour graphics display and a relatively powerful computing engine.

The information revolution that was promised in the 1950s and 1960s with the widespread application of computers has arrived with the World Wide Web. With the WWW the world has shrunk dramatically and our perceptions and methods of data handling and information access have changed. Its impact on education has not yet been dramatic but there is little doubt that the Web will impact teaching and learning strongly in the near future. Those without access to or the ability to use the WWW are already disadvantaged and will become more so as time passes. Technologies are rarely reversible. Once let out of the bottle, there is little that can be done to coax them back in.

Thus the digital divide is first about the WWW, and secondarily about computers and the Internet (viewed in general). It concerns unequal capacity for accessing in a meaningful sense to the resources that the World Wide Web possesses – due either to physical access limitations or to difficulties in controlling communications mechanisms or to inability to understand what is retrieved (*e.g.*, low literacy, unfamiliar language).

WHAT DIFFERENCE DOES THE DIVIDE MAKE?

We care – or should care – about the digital divide because those who are disadvantaged vis-à-vis the WWW will potentially suffer in employment, education, and in their personal lives, as has been described in several of the papers in this same volume. Differential access to the WWW can create differences in grades received in school subjects and differences in acquisition of inquiry skills. There are subtleties, however, to be observed. Low tech skills are required to enable some high tech skills. For example, students can do better writing with a computer than with pen and paper but only if their keyboarding skills are good. A study done at Boston University, using high school students and exam questions patterned after a national writing examination, found that students who had keyboarding skills one half a standard deviation above the mean did better by computer than by hand, while the reverse was found for those with keyboarding skills one half a standard deviation or more below the mean (Russell, 1999).

The general argument to be made is that schools throughout the industrialised world are rapidly moving to incorporate technology and to subscribe to methods of teaching that allow students considerable freedom to search, to explore, and to collaborate with other students. With the skills acquired from these forms of schooling, students will be better prepared for jobs that require technology skills, information searching, and collaboration – jobs that tend to pay quite well – and to be better prepared for college where today computer skills are mandatory. If, as some studies claim, students are more motivated to attend school and to study when they have access to modern computers and the Internet, then a secondary advantage accrues to those within technology rich schools.

The Bangemann Report, which is the foundation of the European Council's action plan for participating in the global information society, includes two educational targets among the ten applications proposed for launching the European information society (Bangemann, 1994). While recognising that "the information society has the potential to improve the quality of life of Europe's citizens, the efficiency of our social and economic organisations and to enforce cohesion", the report also points out the risk of creating a digital divide (*ibid.*, p. 5). "The main risk lies in the creation of a two-tier society of haves and have-nots, in which only a part of the population has access to the new technology, is comfortable using it and can fully enjoy its benefits" (*ibid.*).

Those who sit below the salt

When salt was expensive, it was distributed unequally. The royalty and those they favoured had relatively easy access to it and the rest did not. The round table in the tales of the Knights and the Round Table was significant because when the knights ate, the salt was placed in the middle of the table, thus giving everyone equal access. When persons of unequal rank ate together, a long table was usually used and those of lowest rank placed furthest from the salt. Literally, they sat "below the salt". Comparable to those who sat below the salt are those today who have limited or no WWW access. They sit off-line, disconnected from the WWW. Some of these are unconnected by conscious choice, such as many women and girls; some because they cannott afford to be connected, such as high poverty families and people in rural areas where access is overly expensive; some because they have disabilities that interfere with either physical control of a keyboard or the perception of visual images and text; and some because they cannot interpret the texts due to low literacy or lack of understanding of the language of communication.

Each of these presents a different challenge for eliminating access differences. Some are missing links that need to be constructed, some are wastelands that need to be cultivated and landscaped, and some are foreign languages that need to be learned. Each, in turn, is explored in the following sections.

The missing link

Many people who would like to use the Internet are confronted with access problems. They are ready and willing to connect but some link in the chain that connects from transmitter to receiver is missing. This is what certain classes of disabled people face when trying to get on the WWW as well as some people in remote areas where access is either unavailable or overly expensive. These groups are quite dissimilar otherwise but share an access problem that is external to their own capacities. According to a recent report from the Disability Statistics Center at the University of California-San Francisco, around 50% of all persons in the United States own computers compared to only 24% for the disabled (Greene, 2000). Similarly, about 38% of the total US population uses the Internet compared to about 10% for the disabled.

Schools in the industrialised countries have made considerable progress in the past several decades in making learning more accessible to students with disabilities. Wheel chair ramps, large print books, and the like have made learning easier both in school and out of school for disabled students. Computer technology has offered an even larger potential for assistance, especially for students with motor and communication disabilities. In some schools as well as in many hospitals and other types of health care centres, computer-based assistive devices abound. For those with degenerative nerve diseases, for example, input devices that react to eye movements or even tongue placement are available (Strauss, 1998). However, the dissemination of these devices has not caught up to the demand for them. In addition, some assistive devices are expensive and require special software that limits students who use them to a single machine or to a small number of such machines. Like all other resources, they tend to be more easily available in affluent schools than in less affluent ones.

Not all types of disabilities, however, can be overcome easily with existing assistive devices. For the sight impaired, text-to-speech systems as well as video screen readers are available but their quality still lags for complex Web pages. Speech recognition, a technology that appears to be improving rapidly now, offers considerable advantages for computer input for this group. Nevertheless, it still is expensive and performs quite poorly with continuous speech.

The payoff of the WWW (as well as other Internet based facilities) for the disabled is potentially enormous – relief from social isolation through collaborative learning with e-mail, chat rooms, forums, and the like; access to library resources and other information; on-line instruction; and net-based tutors and mentors – all without having to leave home or school.

A second group of persons affected by the missing link are those in schools in rural areas where convenient access to the Internet is often lacking. For these students satellite and microwave transmission as well as rate reductions such as the E-Rate in the United States are the most practical solutions. Effective access to affordable telecommunications may help schools in remote locations overcome a further inequality resulting from their small enrolments. A small high school may not be able to hire instructors or attract sufficient students for many types of courses that larger high schools offer; *e.g.*, foreign languages, advanced placement, or highly technical subjects. Technology offers a workable solution to this problem through Web-based virtual courses, some of which are already available in a number of countries. Unlike correspondence courses and radio- and video-based instruction, virtual courses on the Web can allow student collaboration, synchronous and asynchronous communications, convenient downloading of instructional resources, and even remote manipulation of laboratory instruments.

A third group affected by the missing link are those from poverty neighbourhoods and those whose schooling is in institutions that draw predominantly from the underclass in a society, which usually means the poor, immigrants, and under-privileged minorities. In the United States, 80 per cent of the first-year students at private universities used e-mail during 1998 while at public, historically Black colleges, only 41 per cent did (Gladieux and Swail, 1999). At the elementary and secondary levels similar inequalities also exist. In 1998, 57 per cent of the instructional rooms within public and private schools with less than 6 per cent minority students enrolled were connected to the Internet, yet only 37 per cent of the instructional rooms in schools with 50% or more minority students were.

A more recent report from the National Center on Education Statistics, a division of the U.S. Department of Education, shows that in the spring of 1999, 52% of the teachers in low poverty schools (defined as having fewer than 11% of the students eligible for free or reduced-price school lunch) used computers and the Internet "a lot" to create instructional materials while only 32% of the teachers in high poverty schools (71% or more of the students eligible for free or reduced-price school lunch) did so. Similar differences also occurred for using computers and the Internet for administrative record keeping and for communicating with colleagues (NCES, 2000). These differences probably result from differences in technical equipment and support, training in the use of ICT, and the school culture related to ICT.

It should be observed, nevertheless, that the inequalities in most countries within schools are far smaller than those found outside of schools, that is, within communities and homes. Furthermore, in most of the industrialised countries, a high percentage of the classrooms in all schools will soon be technology supplied. This will not eliminate inequalities based upon other factors such as teacher preparedness for integrating ICT into instruction, but it will reduce the size of the gap between schools in low income areas and those in high ones.

Nevertheless, school children in poorer urban neighbourhoods have two potential access problems. One is in the school itself, where, as cited above, technology access is rarely equal to that of the schools in more affluent areas. But another barrier is found in the community and home support system for academic ICT use. In the more affluent areas there are more computers and Internet connections available outside of school for supporting homework, and more technical expertise for correcting problems that might occur. To overcome these problems in the United Kingdom, the ministers of E-Commerce and of Technology have jointly suggested wiring Internet connections in schools, churches, and bars in poor urban areas as an approach to exposing people in deprived neighbourhoods to the Internet (Pastore, 2000). In the United States, President Clinton has proposed a $100 million programme to create 1 000 Community Technology Centers in low-income urban and rural neighbourhoods (Clinton, 2000).

In Singapore, the Infocomm Development Authority has committed $25 million to a programme to bring affordable and accessible computers and Internet connections to 30 000 low income households, along with technology training. The object is to allow lower-income families access to the same computing resources that students from more affluent homes have through their own equipment and service provider subscriptions. Free broadband access to the Internet will also be offered to community centres and clubs (Nisperos, 2000). Teachers in Singapore have noticed that students with access to the Internet outside of school are able to download images and other types of information that allow them to earn higher grades. In addition, these pupils are acquiring more advanced inquiry skills.

The wasteland

Many women and girls view the world of computing as a wasteland, according to a recent report from the American Association of University Women (AAUW, 2000). A co-chair of the Commission that drafted the report concluded that "Girls are critical of the computer culture, not computer phobic" (AAUW, 2000, p. 1). Women, who make up over 50% of the US college enrolment, receive about 9% of the engineering-related bachelors degrees, less than 28% of the computer science bachelor degrees, and represent only 17% of those who take the computer science advanced placement test. Among information technology professionals, women are about 20% of the total.

The Commission found that programming classes were perceived by girls to be tedious and dull, computer games "boring, redundant, and violent, and computer career options uninspiring" (*ibid.*, p. 1f). To remedy this situation, the Commission recommended a number of steps for schools and communities, including changing the public face of computing so that women will not perceive it as solitary and antisocial; transforming software so that it appeals to a wider range of people and does not reinforce the "computer nerd" stereotype; preparing tech-savvy teachers who can teach how to use computers as productivity tools; and providing opportunities for girls to express their technological imaginations.

A wasteland also separates college training in the information technology field in the United States and two large minority groups there: African-Americans and Hispanics. For example, only about two per cent of all undergraduate computer science degrees were awarded in 1998 to these two groups, respectively, and only 10 of those receiving Ph.D.'s that same year were African-Americans and only 6 were Hispanics, out of a total of about 950 degrees received (Becht *et al.*, 1999). (At the undergraduate level, African-Americans represent 10.5% of the total US citizen enrolment and Hispanics, 8.1%.)

Whether this problem is a function of a wasteland that potentially could be made more inviting or belongs more in the foreign language category is difficult to determine. The majority of those students who major in computer sciences at the university level were probably identified as advanced in mathematics before the end of elementary school. The probability of such talent being recognised and fostered in schools drawing from high poverty areas, where a high percentage of African-Americans and Hispanics live, is not as high as for the same ability level in schools drawing from more affluent areas. If the problem begins at this level (or earlier), changes to hardware and software will have little impact on reducing it.

The foreign language

Simply wiring schools or neighbourhood organisations to the Internet does not guarantee that effective use of ICT will occur. For many, computers and the

Internet represent, metaphorically and actually, a foreign language that they do not speak or understand. Janet Schofield and her colleagues have documented many of the non-technical barriers to using the Internet effectively in schools, including mismatches in schedules, goals, and norms (Schofield and Davidson, 1998). These problems result from a failure to understand the Internet and the conditions under which it is most effectively used for learning. More importantly, many students lack experience not only in technically-based skills but also in information handling and in effective independent learning. For these students a range of skills need to be taught, including self-monitoring and time management, before computers and the Internet become intelligible.

Unlike television and radio, the Internet requires active, autonomous engagement to realise its full benefits. Stored information is available, as well as connections to dynamic information sources, including real-time data (*e.g.*, weather satellite transmissions) and advisors, tutors, mentors, and the like. But all of these require active search, communication, and information management skills, as well as constant monitoring to extract from the overwhelming bulk of texts, diagrams, tables, photographs, and the like what is needed for a given task or assignment. Those students who have good self-monitoring skills and are highly motivated to learn usually do better in independent learning than those who do not (Heckhausen and Dweck, 1998; Schunk and Zimmerman, 1994).

The association of educational ICT with constructivist approaches to learning, although often overplayed, derives from the potential that ICT has for implementing active and collaborative learning. Simulations, case-based teaching, cross-national discussion and debate, and the like are all facilitated by the Internet in particular. For these approaches to work productively, however, teachers must shift from lecturing and micro-managing activity and discussion to guiding learning through more and more independent student engagements with other students and with extra-classroom resources (Jonassen *et al.,* 1999). The ideal instructional mixture for K-12 schooling will vary according to student age and maturity level but will always involve a combination of direct instruction, guided and independent practice, group interaction, and individual reflection, search, and creation. Some teachers already teach this way and can, through acquisition of technology skills, integrate ICT easily into their teaching. Others need to acquire both new teaching styles and the requisite technology skills.

A less tractable problem is presented by those with low literacy and inadequate language skills for the languages of wider communication used within a country. Much of the value of the WWW rests in text and technical diagrams that are at or above high school reading level. Students who enter secondary school still reading at a far lower level will gain little meaning from most of what they encounter on the WWW. Similarly, those who do not command the language of the WWW materials will also have limited access to content. Although smart text-to-speech systems could serve the low literacy audience along with the blind, the low literacy group often has difficulties with listening comprehension due to vocabulary deficits. For those who do not comprehend the language of wider communication, translation systems are a possible relief. However, systems are currently in development primarily for the major world languages – Spanish, German, French, English, Russian – and so far lack the reliability required for educational applications. Some school systems are placing a stronger emphasis than ever before on second language learning, particularly English, to ensure that students will be able to use the WWW profitably.

To understand what national policies might work to close the digital divide for those affected by the foreign language problem, we must first develop a working model of how ICT impacts student abilities. One such model is shown in the figure below, using the development of ICT skills as the dependent variable. This model assumes that three factors feed directly into this ability: school ICT use, home ICT use, and student capacity for self-learning. In turn, school ICT use is controlled by teacher ICT ability, school ICT resources, and school academic standards. Home ICT use is not further analysed, but might be viewed as a function of resources, technology assistance, and attitudes toward learning.

Student capacity for self-learning is important for ICT skill acquisition because of the nature of computing as a solitary activity, particularly for middle and secondary grade levels, as well as the high demand for problem solving caused by the current state of the technologies: system crashes, incompatibilities across file formats, inaccurate or opaque instruction manuals, and so on. Hativa (1988), for example, has found that differences in self-study ability are a major contribution to the widening of the performance gap that occurs when computer-assisted instruction is used for mathematics. Students who can monitor their own learning, recognise when they are not understanding a concept, seek help, and communicate their learning needs to others tend to learn more from a self-paced system than those who are weak in these abilities.

School ICT use is the area where national policies can have their most direct impact. However, much more than hardware, software, and networking is required. Besides assuring that all schools have modern equipment and technological support, policy must also be directed at teacher training and at school standards. Model teacher training projects for ICT skills can be found in a number of countries, including Ireland, the Netherlands, Singapore, and the United Kingdom. A proposed Mexican effort is of special interest because it is part of a larger strategy to use ICT to promote school reform and involves a large element of participation by teachers in planning, courseware development, and instructional support. The UK project has been built around laptops and Internet service accounts provided at reduced costs to teachers who receive ICT training (BECTA, 1998).

The development of student ICT skills – A causal mapping

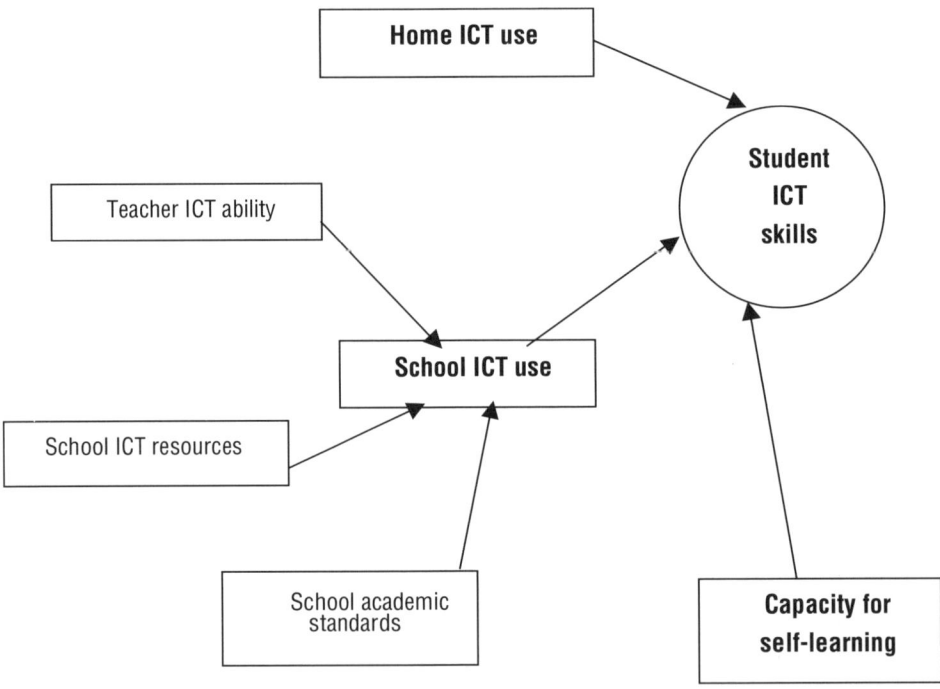

In contrast to the assumptions of even 10 years ago about the role of ICT in schooling, the modern view is that the teacher's ability to integrate ICT into the curriculum is critical to the successful use of ICT by students. This is a radical change from the past where computer-assisted instruction (CAI) and integrated learning systems (ILS) were viewed as answers within themselves and little need was seen to prepare teachers in ICT skills. The further step needed to make courseware effective for all students is for publishers to focus on providing resources for teachers to integrate in their lessons rather than full on-line courses that attempt to duplicate what teachers do. The resources that are most needed are those that centre on topics that are difficult to teach – the water cycle and electrical conductivity in science, place value in basic arithmetic operations, comprehension of conditional phrases in reading, and so on. If there is a true added value to full colour animation, real-time data, hypertext, diagnostic networks, and the like, then it will show up best in those areas where teachers typically have the most difficulties rather than in areas where teaching is less challenging.

The role of school academic standards in student ICT skill acquisition has been largely ignored, yet looms as large as equipment differences in the skill acquisition equation. Schools that have high standards encourage their students to do more sophisticated learning with ICT than schools with lower standards. In the lower standards settings, students might use word processors and spread sheets for mundane tasks, and occasionally search the World Wide Web for information, using simple searches and a single search engine. In schools with higher standards, students use spreadsheets to simulate different planting options in agriculture or policy options in government, build their own Web pages, and manage forums. When they search the WWW, they use complex searches and a variety of different search engines.

Policies for improving home computing for school-age students can be modelled on a number of successful projects world-wide. The Singapore home computing effort is one such project as is the Buddy project in the United States that supplies equipment, training and support services for parents of school-age children. Some factors related to home computing are more difficult to equalise. For example, in many countries wealthy neighbourhoods are upgraded with modern, high speed Internet lines while low income neighbourhoods are left with inferior communication equipment, if any at all. National policies to eliminate these disparities will be more difficult to formulate because the private sector is often involved.

The College Board report cited earlier has other recommendations for avoiding a wider digital divide in virtual campuses and in other technology-based academic programmes. For designers, they suggested placing access at the core of system design, keeping the promise of technology in perspective by balancing traditional and technology-based delivery, and learning from the distance-learning pioneers. For the communications industry, they suggest more social responsibility, reflected in consideration of how to stimulate broad access when developing products and services (Gladieux and Swail, 1999).

SUMMARY

The digital divide in formal schooling is not simply an equipment differential that can be overcome with further selective investments in hardware, software, and networking. Instead it derives from both within school and within home differences that extend to learning standards as well as support. Student self-learning ability, and in particular, student ability for independent learning, is an additional factor. National policies that attempt to close the digital divide for schooling must attend to all of these contributing factors to be successful.

Not discussed here are differences across even the highly industrialised countries in computer ownership and in use of the Internet, factors that impact schooling and learning. For example, while almost 37 per cent of the Swedish population has used the Internet this past year (1999), only about 26 per cent of the Danish population has and only about 10 per cent of the Italian. Within the European Union these differences may, in time, become important, especially as students become more mobile and courses and programmes more global.

Efforts to eliminate digital differences need to continue along all fronts: assistive devices, including speech recognition for the disabled, low cost communications for schools in remote areas, redesign of both hardware and software for women and girls, and more training for teachers, more technical assistance for parents, and more academic supports for students from high poverty and language minority backgrounds. The digital divide in formal schooling is not a single problem that can be fixed with a programme of massive school aid and technological supports. Instead it is, in part, a function of a lack of specific types of resources and in part of chronic differences that will not yield to any single remediation. These latter problems are a continuing reminder of the basic inequalities of most modern societies. ICT, if appropriately deployed, could contribute in more than a small way to alleviating these problems; employed differently may only exacerbate them.

CHAPTER 6
Basic Skills in Adult Education and the Digital Divide
by
Lynda Ginsburg, John Sabatini and Daniel A. Wagner[18]

INTRODUCTION

Traditionally, basic adult education has had a particular concern with the skills of literacy and numeracy, seeing these as essential for entry to the world of work. Adult education teachers may therefore be reluctant to adopt ICT, unsure of the part it should play, and worried about the time it takes away from the development of those basic skills. As we enter the 21st century, however, ICT has already become a necessary and important component of adult education. Formal and non-formal education are being delivered at a distance via technology – particularly the Internet – with the promise that learning can take place at any time and in any place.

Moreover, technology may provide the motivation that draws into adult education those who might otherwise not participate, and facilitate more meaningful learning for them. With all the talk about the *information*

18. Lynda Ginsberg and John Sabatini, Senior Researchers, NCAL, University of Pennsylvania; Daniel A. Wagner, Director and Professor at NCAL, and Director, International Literacy Institute.

superhighway, many people feel the need for *driving lessons* so as not to get left by the roadside. Whereas those who lack reading, writing and mathematical skills are likely to be embarrassed by their inability, the same appears not to be as true for those who have yet to master technology skills. It is the ability to use ICT that is now seen as integral to obtaining and keeping jobs in almost every sector of industrialised economies. One has only to think, for instance, of the procedures for entering data in a business, hospital or restaurant, producing a shipping inventory in a factory or delivering a package.

According to the U.S. Department of Commerce (NTIA, 1999), disparities in access to ICT in America are significantly related to race, income and education demographics. For example, Black and Hispanic households are less than half as likely as white households to have Internet access. Families with an income over $75 000 are more than 4 times as likely to have a computer at home – and more than 6 times as likely to have home Internet access – as those with an income under $20 000 (over 20 million U.S. households). Also, households with higher levels of education among adults are far more likely to own computers and have Internet access than those at the lowest education levels, as the table indicates:

Household level of education among adults	Households possessing personal computers, %
No more than elementary education	8
Some high school education	16
High school diploma or equivalent	31

How many individuals in the United States and in other industrialised OECD countries have these levels of education? The U.S. National Adult Literacy Survey (Kirsch *et al.*, 1993) estimated that 40 to 44 million adult Americans, which is nearly 25% of the working population, have literacy scores in the lowest proficiency level. Similar findings have been reported in other OECD countries (OECD/Statistics Canada, 1995, 1997). About 45 million American adults do not have a high school diploma or General Education Development (GED) equivalent certificate (GEDTS, 1998), yet only 4 million of them participate annually in programmes to improve their basic reading skills and further their educational prospects.

Adults in the United States with low literacy – and in other OECD countries and many developing countries – are heterogeneous demographically, with large variations in ethnicity and language background, such as immigrants (Wagner *et al.,* 1999). Increasing numbers of studies in industrialised countries show that bio-behavioural factors, such as dyslexia, poor eyesight and learning disabilities, may affect literacy acquisition (Wagner and Venezky, 1999). Such individuals, like most adults, may have complex family, work, and social circumstances that cannot easily be put aside to permit education to take place, so adult literacy programmes typically have high drop-in and drop-out rates. These factors add additional complexity to issues of instruction methods, learning strategies, and programme planning and management.

In this chapter we suggest that the digital divide among adults within and across many nations is likely to persist for some years, the adults concerned being probably more resistant to change than children and youth, who will be growing up within societies ever more permeated by new technologies. Furthermore, up to the present the vast majority of ICT investment in education worldwide has gone into statutory schools and higher education, without regard for the educational needs of disadvantaged adults. There are extraordinary opportunities for ICT to bring about significant change for adult populations with low literacy, especially since adult education is less hampered by rigid education systems, required curricula, and constraints on individual motivation. The greater the divide or gap, the more dramatic the leap can be. In non-formal adult education, these leaps are only now beginning. Most of the examples in this chapter are drawn from the United States, where the focus on new ICT for adults is relatively advanced.

TECHNOLOGY SKILLS AND ADULT LEARNING

Whether in Tucson, Turin or Timbuktu, adults come to non-formal adult education programmes with a diverse range of needs and interests, along with a considerable array of skills, dispositions and experiences. The programmes are normally voluntary in nature, with individuals deciding whether to attend and how often. Participation may meet a workplace requirement, reflect an interest in learning skills not previously acquired, or be motivated by wanting to be able to support their own children's education. The key questions for ICT are its role in encouraging participation, and how it can help adult learners achieve their goals.

It is important to understand that definitions of literacy and basic skills needs are changing rapidly in most countries (Tuijnman *et al.*, 1997). Sufficient reading and mathematical skills are no longer enough; *technological literacy* (the ability to utilise ICT effectively) is becoming an additional educational necessity. Entry to further education or training courses may assume the skills, preparation, levels of commitment, and experience normally acquired by the end of secondary school. Increasingly for school leavers these skills will include familiarity and competence with ICT. It follows that mature adults who completed their studies before the advent of educational ICT will find themselves at a major disadvantage, when seeking entry to such courses. Let us look briefly at several domains where adult life intersects with technology and education.

The world of work

In the early 1990s, the U.S. Department of Labor set out to define general workplace skills that American workers need for a growing and changing economy (SCANS, 1991). Although different professions require different specific skills, most demand a set of basic competencies. Researchers set out to identify these foundational requirements, by interviewing employers, trainers and workers from several industries. Technology was identified separately within the enquiry, but technological competency was found to have permeated all skill areas, including the management of resources, communication with colleagues, and the acquisition and use of information.

An additional consideration for success in a quickly-changing work environment is the ability to continuously upgrade and master new skills, whether in response to shifting workplace priorities, obsolescence of job functions, or the implementation of new technologies. Since ICT is frequently at the centre of such changes, those who lack technological literacy skills find their options and opportunities to be restricted (Ginsburg and Elmore, 1998). In addition, the workers able to use today's technologies are the ones best equipped to learn the technologies of tomorrow.

Home and family

Many adults are motivated to return to education as they realise their limitations in regard to helping their children with school work. Schools are increasingly using ICT, thereby leaving parents who are unfamiliar with technology less able to support their children's education than they would have been a generation earlier. In addition, parents may need to negotiate on behalf of their children, for instance over testing and placement for learning disabilities or exceptional abilities, and in the United States will find that parental information, support groups, and even legal advice, are available via the Internet. There is a gap in awareness of, and access to, these information resources.

Technological change is affecting what it means to function successfully in everyday life. The increasing automation in financial activities is having a major impact on how the average American household manages its fiscal affairs, from paying bills to investing in the stock market. Making decisions about medical treatment can be informed by perusing the extensive medical research and support networks available on the Internet, and encounters with the medical system are increasingly automated – both in record keeping and in medical care. Already many millions of citizens are using the Internet in this fashion.

Technology's potential impact on adult education

Those who dropped out of school often come to adult education with a history of frustrating and negative educational experiences, with expectations of failure and fears that structured adult learning will mean more of the same. They may describe earlier schooling as boring, rigid, alienating and insensitive. Many teachers in the adult education service might be sympathetic, but their curriculum and classroom styles have too often been those remembered from earlier schooldays. In one of the most dramatic pedagogical changes of the past decade, teachers can now use technology to create classroom experiences that more readily reflect present-day realities. Learners can develop the literacy, numeracy, problem solving, and technology skills that are actually used in every day life. For many this kind of instruction is empowering rather than frustrating, engaging rather than boring, and more obviously useful, especially in terms of job outcomes.

In addition, by employing ICT, teachers can individualise instruction. Until quite recently, the only resources available to most adult literacy courses were sets of workbooks, often a small library of books for learners to read, and perhaps newspapers, magazines, dictionaries and other reference books. Some teachers brought in additional resources for particular activities aimed at engaging learners. Now, however, computers with Internet connections can provide access in the classroom to a seemingly limitless repository of information, ideas and resources, as well as opportunities to communicate with people all over the world. Learners can themselves participate in the design of learning activities to accommodate areas of personal interest. Interactive software is becoming available in an increasing number of languages, and immigrants are able to find out what is happening in their home countries.

The integration of technology into adult education also changes the classroom culture. Some teachers and learners find the changes in the roles and relative power dynamics of the teacher and learners exciting, while others see them to be disconcerting and confusing. Learners have access to a greater variety and depth of information independent of the teacher, who no longer has to specify all classroom activities, but may become a facilitator who questions, encourages, helps, and challenges. Learners take more control and responsibility for their own learning. As yet, however, only small number of programmes in a few countries are actively implementing this model of adult learning. Neither in the United States, nor in other industrialised or developing countries, can we say that technology-based adult education has yet become the *modus operandi*, but we can suggest this is the direction for the future.

KEY FACTORS IN THE DEVELOPMENT OF ICT-BASED ADULT EDUCATION

In the United States and other industrialised countries, the average per capita annual expenditure on adult education is less than 10% of that spent on formal schooling for children, and in developing countries (where the needs are even greater) the percentage drops to as little as one per cent (Wagner, 1995). Adult literacy programmes have poorer Internet access than public schools (NCES, 1999):

	U.S. adult literacy programmes	U.S. public schools
Internet access	50	89
Classrooms connected	40	51

Moreover, only about half of these programmes with Internet access had high-capacity lines, which puts adult education at the *have-not* end of the digital spectrum.

Facilities and access

One way to conceptualise the challenges of the digital divide for adult learning is to look at the issue of access to facilities and infrastructure. In the United States, many states hold adult classes in school or community college facilities, which largely reduces the access problem to that of competing for available time. Since many adult education classes are held during evenings, weekends, and other non-schooling periods, significant access is possible. Another strategy often chosen by large volunteer tutoring programmes, is to use community centres such as public libraries or job centres as the centre for ICT. Those individuals who are least likely to have Internet access at home or work (earning less than $20 000 per year, minority groups, and those without a college degree), rely most on ICT resources in public facilities (NTIA, 1999). The promotion of community learning centres may also be seen in Europe, Asia and Africa (for one interesting example in Ghana, see Fontaine and Foote, 1999).

Home access to the Internet has become more and more popular, even in relatively poor communities in industrialised countries, though less so in developing countries. In the United States, learning at home with public broadcasting of learning materials has helped over a million adults to obtain the General Education Development (GED) equivalent of the secondary school qualification. Other broadcasts – such as *Crossroads Café* – have targeted basic skills and English as a Second Language. These television programmes, viewed live or on video, are important for populations unable to attend adult education classes. Home learning resources and programmes are now beginning to move towards multi-media and web-based delivery, as described further below.

Teaching and learning

In order to promote ICT-based learning, it is necessary to demonstrate the availability of high quality, cost-effective technology-based curricula, and to prepare teachers to use these materials, through an affordable professional development programme. Several recent large-scale initiatives have begun developing multimedia curricula and instructional materials geared to the needs of adult learners, including the federally-funded *LiteracyLink* and *CLASS* projects described below. These resources and curricula can be used as a comprehensive programme or can be integrated with other instructional materials and activities.

Adult educators frequently feel unprepared to use technology, being unable to fall back on well-developed models from their own learning experiences. They have few informal opportunities to learn from each other or to share teaching resources. Many of them – only now becoming technologically literate – are just beginning to explore the myriad of Internet sites that contain lesson plans and technology-rich instructional activities. They face the problems of how to manage classroom activities with only one computer, or to be sure that learners are progressing in reading, writing, and mathematics if they are using the Internet. Where can they get ideas for instructional activities that work for adult learners? How can they deal with learners who are at different levels of literacy, and what happens when they are asked questions that they cannot answer? It is important to address these issues. High quality professional development opportunities are needed for adult education teachers to become confident and competent users of ICT.

PROGRAMMES THAT BRIDGE THE DIGITAL DIVIDE

Access to ICT-based learning at home

In the United States, two promising programmes are aimed at helping traditionally under-served families to gain home-based access to ICT and opportunities to learn. One, LINCT,[19] seeks to help communities achieve electronic equity through a locally-managed learn-and-earn process. The communities co-operate with corporations, to generate a sustainable supply of donated, recyclable technology, and to provide ICT trainers. In South Phoenix, Arizona, low-income families can "buy" their own home computer, following 100 hours of service on the programme as a tutor, a tutee or a tutor supervisor. LINCT provides training and has reported evidence of participants developing literacy and numeracy skills. The *Time Dollars* earned from this participation may be used to "purchase" a refurbished computer and subsequently computer up-grades, modems and peripheral up-grades. Exceptional participants, provided with 300 hours of technology training over 12 weeks, become paid employees of the programme.[20]

A second programme is *Neighborhood Networks*, that offers access to advanced technology, with training and support, to help residents increase their earning power and move off welfare and other public subsidies. Seed capital is provided to establish computer centres in privately-owned apartment buildings. The centres are sustained financially by contributions from local partners in each community and by income generated from the centres' own business initiatives. They offer welfare-to-work initiatives, classes in General Education Development (GED) high-school equivalent qualifications, basic computer-literacy training, resume

---

19. The LINCT Coalition, Learning and Information Networking for Community – via Telecomputing.

20. See http//www.linct.org.

writing, with use of computers in a home-based environment that is convenient for families. Parents can acquire skills that increase their employment marketability, while children can use the technology for school projects (Neighborhood Networks, 1998).

Support for adult educators

Two resources, *LitTeacher*[21] and *Captured Wisdom*,[22] are newly available to help adult literacy teachers develop their own technology skills and methodology for integrating ICT into learning programmes. *LitTeacher* is a virtual resource centre, which includes training in technology issues, technology assistance, a menu of materials on literacy education, a wide assortment of existing literacy resources and professional development video conferences. The virtual centre assists literacy teachers and service providers in making effective use of curriculum materials, and enables the development of electronic communities of teachers for mutual support and learning.

Captured Wisdom is an interactive resource designed to allow adult educators to visit colleagues' classrooms virtually, to see successful practices of integrating technology into adult education. Disseminated in videotape and CD-ROM formats to adult literacy programmes across the United States, *Captured Wisdom* provides the adult educational community with inspiration into what ICT can accomplish. Experienced teachers and learners were filmed using technology in classroom-based, replicable projects that support learning in traditional and new content areas. The videotaped segments were viewed by focus groups of teachers who generated questions about the practices and techniques described. These questions were grouped into categories such as *Classroom Management*, *Assessment*, *Technical Issues*, and were posed to the presenting teacher, whose responses were recorded and included. The classroom-based projects serve as springboards for discussions about how such projects and teaching techniques can be adapted to suit individual teaching styles, learners' needs and local education contexts.

---

21. *LitTeacher* is a component of the *LiteracyLink* Project [a US Department of Education funded partnership of the Public Broadcasting Service, Kentucky Educational Television, National Center on Adult Literacy (NCAL) at the University of Pennsylvania, and the Kentucky Department of Education].

22. *Captured Wisdom*, developed by the federally-funded North Central Regional Technology in Education Consortium for K-12 teachers, was extended to adult literacy educators by the National Center on Adult Literacy (NCAL).

Helping adult learners prepare for the 21st century workplace

Two other American programmes are helping adult learners to work with the technology that is used in the workplace. The Central Illinois Adult Education Service Center (http://www.cait.org/ciaesc) has developed an intensive 60-hour pilot programme during which adults who have been on public assistance prepare themselves to enter the workforce. Each learner creates an electronic portfolio, that includes examples of work prepared with the various software application packages used in most businesses. In addition, learners create an electronic "All about me" presentation, employing software that can be used to demonstrate their capabilities during a job interview. The ICT skills acquired are not insignificant, but of even more note is the new air of confidence instilled, as participants realise they are learning what many better educated adults have not yet begun to master.

Rend Lake College (http://www.rlc.cc.il.us/Skills) adult education teachers have created project-based learning materials for their GED secondary equivalent qualification. Packets have been prepared filled with the minutiae of an imaginary work environment, including biographies and timesheets of individual employees, complaints from unsatisfied customers, orders and financial information. Learners are charged with acting as consultants, to make recommendations to save the business. They may use technology as they think appropriate, whether to write letters, prepare budgets with spreadsheets, or find marketing information on the Internet. This enables them to acquire meaningful workplace skills, while at the same time developing the reading, writing and numeracy skills that they need to complete their high school equivalent certificate.

Opportunities for independent learning

The CLASS project[23] (http://class.unl.edu/final_web/index.html) aims to develop and operate a system that provides on-line, nationwide access to educational and curriculum resources, including the support services necessary for students to acquire a fully accredited high school diploma. When completed in 2001, CLASS will have 54 accredited courses available to students. The scheme provides an alternative to traditional class work, tailored to those students who may need special consideration from the non-traditional, geographically

---

23. The CLASS *Project* (Communications, Learning, and Assessment in a Student-centred System) is a partnership of the Independent Study High School at the University of Nebraska-Lincoln, and the Nebraska Department of Education.

isolated or disadvantaged segments of the population, including the gifted as well as at-risk learners. It offers an alternative to learners who did not complete high school, regardless of their age or situation, and supplements the work and course selection of any student wishing to pursue topics that are not available in their current learning setting. Availability extends widely, for instance to those who work during the day, those who are home-bound for a variety of reasons, or those serving time in prison. Students can work on the programme whenever they wish, and devote to it as much time as they need.

The *LiteracyLink* initiative (http://www.pbs.org/literacy) is also designed to use print resources, ICT and the Internet, to help adults receive literacy instruction and gain a high school diploma or GED equivalent. It includes the production and distribution of new video materials, that can be delivered by broadcast television or video tape. There are 26 video programmes for *Workplace Essential Skills* (WES), addressing basic skills in a workplace context – reading, writing, communication and mathematics. WES also addresses issues of job searching, career planning, and workplace culture orientation. The videos are complemented by on-line and printed material. *LitLearner* on-line integrates the video and other Internet resources in easy-to-use electronic formats, with icon-driven menus.

Another component, *LitHelper*, will help students and teachers to tailor the video, print, and on-line instructional materials to specific students or to local literacy programmes. It includes both assessment and management functions to help the learner and teacher manage their learning. Special website "tours" are used to introduce learners to the on-line system. *LitHelper* will also provide personal appraisals to give a better sense of the most appropriate activities to match the learners' specific needs. All learner on-line interactions are collected in a personal *HomeSpace*, that includes portfolio functions for on-going assessment of progress and periodic revisions of the learning plan.

ADULT LEARNING AND ICT IN RICH AND POOR COUNTRIES

We noted earlier that, to varying degrees, improved literacy and basic skills are a recognised need in all countries, rich and poor. In all countries economic growth and civic participation depend increasingly on an educated community. In this chapter, we have focused primarily on ICT and adult learning in the United States, as that is the locus of some of the most innovative projects to date. While many countries around the world are beginning to invest significantly in ICT for school-aged populations, relatively little as yet has been undertaken for disadvantaged adults (in contrast with adults learning in the university). Given the chronic under-funding of adult education in general, it may be no surprise that ICT investment has been thought too expensive, especially in developing countries. However, unless adult education is equipped to take advantage of the tremendous potential of network technologies and distance education, the gap between the information-rich and the information-poor will continue to grow.

We know that the penetration of the Internet is increasing across the different socio-economic groups in industrialised countries. It is extending also across poorer developing countries – though often superficially as yet – as evidenced by *Internet cafés* sprouting up in the street in such countries around the globe. One can get connected from nearly any urban or semi-urban location worldwide. The impact of such access for adult education in developing countries is not yet known, as many of these countries lack the resources for adult literacy programmes and campaigns.

Effective development in adult education – as in other educational sectors – requires of necessity a primary focus on improving the professional development of teachers and the utilisation of distance-education methods. Teachers are the main, but also the most expensive resource of education worldwide. To an extent, attention to this professional development has begun in the formal schooling sector, but relatively little has been done in adult education. However, the International Literacy Institute (UNESCO-affiliated) at the University of Pennsylvania has now completed a prototype of *International Literacy Explorer*, a teacher-training multimedia tool for basic educators (Wagner, 2000). In a public/private partnership called *Bridges to the Future*, ILI and NCAL are working to adapt such multi-media tools for the professional development of adult educators in a number of developing countries (see ILI/NCAL website: www.literacy.org).

CONCLUSION

It is not unreasonable to expect that in only a few years, ICT (especially personal computers and the Internet) will have reached a saturation level among the United States population similar to that of telephones and television. Computers will be found in homes and in public access sites across the country. Perhaps a system of universal service for homes will be put into place, in the way that the federal e-rate programme provides subsidies to impoverished schools to help them get to the technology levels of wealthier schools. Even if everyone had such access to ICT, important questions would remain.

Will adults (in addition to school children and youth) take advantage of the learning opportunities available through ICT, or as with television, will entertainment and shopping win out over learning?   Thus far, the use of ICT relies heavily on written communication.   Will those who have limited literacy skills be left behind even when ICT is easily accessible, because they cannot read and write well enough to benefit from it?

We know that only a small percentage of those who could benefit actually enter adult education programmes, and many do not participate for long enough for any meaningful impact. Improving the ways technology is utilised as a learning tool can make adult education more engaging and more effective. Already ICT is providing additional opportunities to learn in less structured environments, such as independently at home or at libraries. It remains to be seen if the numbers opting for such alternative educational routes will increase, as the technology becomes more available and more user friendly.

As we have noted, ICT-based education seems to be ideal for giving additional educational opportunities to at-risk and disadvantaged adult learners, but research is urgently needed to identify best approaches for helping them to succeed in these new learning environments.

CHAPTER 7
Towards Bridging Learning's Digital Divide
Synthesis by the OECD Secretariat

INTRODUCTION

As in Chapter 4, this chapter summarises the relevant Roundtable discussion and documentation other than the major presentations. It does so through a focus on relationships and strategies relevant to the digital divide in education and learning, the earlier synthesis concentrating on the divide itself. It examines general policy dilemmas, the relationships involved in marrying the aims of quality and equity as the use of ICT for learning extends more widely, and the roles of stakeholders in the process. In conclusion there is discussion of issues relating to the value of the international exchange of experiences and evaluation. As with the earlier synthesis, the chapter's sources mean that it is selective rather than comprehensive.

TENSIONS AND DILEMMAS

It would be convenient if the policy issues related to the digital divide could be understood as a set of recipes for improvement, which countries could implement to a greater or lesser degree. It is clear, however, that the reality is more complex and dynamic than any simple model allows. Dilemmas abound. They arise in relation to the very aims and outcomes of learning, linked as they are with economic and social well-being, for while the inter-connections are frequently characterised positively in terms of the *knowledge society*, they have a powerful negative side. The consequences for individuals, organisations or communities of falling behind in learning become the more profound, and can be dire. The process of creating *winners* often creates *losers*.

Dilemmas arise in relation to extending opportunities for lifelong learning, especially individualised forms of learning that exploit ICT in different ways. There is a growing complexity of learning provision and decision-making, involving formal or non-formal settings and public, private or mixed arrangements. The complexity can heighten the barriers to participation of those not well equipped for the knowledge society. Seen in this light, lifelong learning can be regarded not only as part of the *solution* but as an integral part of the *problem*. Account should be taken, therefore, of the negative consequences for the most disadvantaged, as the general levels of ICT expertise and learning complexity continue to rise.

Parallel dilemmas occur in relation to the specific goal of improving ICT competence, and the high priority this now receives among educational objectives. On the one hand, the importance of technologies in today's knowledge-based societies justifies such a high priority (Chapters 8 and 9 give illustrations of how prominent technology goals have become in national educational policy strategies). On the other hand, this very prominence makes the exclusion faced by those who still miss out the more acute. Policy strategies are needed to extend ICT access for learning and competence as widely as possible, with particular attention to those whose disadvantages are most acute.

Equity and quality – Approaches and stakeholders

Focusing on the digital divide is first and foremost to highlight considerations of *equity* in terms of opportunity and access. These considerations are easily overlooked, in the enthusiasm to open new horizons in learning and teaching via technology to those most ready to embrace them – students, teachers, institutions and communities – who are often, but not always, already relatively advantaged. At the same time, a great deal of Roundtable attention focused on issues relating to *quality*, in relation to ICT materials and learning environments. Some have supposed the pursuit of quality and the pursuit of equity to be in conflict, as though more of one can only be achieved at the expense of the other. As the Roundtable discussion underlined, however, these issues are inextricably intertwined and both are integral to addressing the digital divide.

Problems relating to the quality of ICT learning materials were highlighted by several Roundtable participants. There is the need for educational software production to be seen as a priority rather than as an "add-on" to the hardware, and for contents to be of the highest quality. Too often ICT learning materials are of poor quality – whether on-line or not – which is especially problematic for those whose needs are greatest. Nevertheless, several participants expressed a caution about ICT *tools*, since attempts to market versions specific to education had not succeeded. In any case, educational ICT applications – such as word processing – should wherever possible be based on the non-education-specific software that learners will meet in other contexts, such as the office or the home.

For the implementation of educational ICT strategies to bridge different divides, the position of the teacher is seen to be pivotal. By the same token, poorly prepared or unmotivated teachers can exercise a strong negative influence and thereby reinforce divides. One participant expressed the challenge with urgency: "we have no choice but to get teachers up to speed". Teacher education and professional development considerations should thus be to the fore in ICT learning initiatives, with a dual emphasis required. First, professional development is needed to build teachers' ICT confidence and competence, including their knowledge of educational applications. Second, there is need to change teaching styles, moving away from didactic methods and towards tutoring and supported learning. There is value in focusing on networks of teachers, to get beyond the isolated endeavours of individual enthusiasts, and to foster the likelihood of change becoming firmly embedded in the ethos and practice of the different educational institutions involved. However, although major teacher training programmes have been initiated, and information resources created for teachers and students, the scale of provision is as yet not matched to the need:

> "The neglect of teacher ICT training, which tends to lag behind physical investment, is often considered a major obstacle… In the United States, it is remarkable that expenditure on technology training for instructional staff increased only slightly from 4% of the technology budget in 1994-95 to 5% in 1998-99, given the high political priority of the use of ICT in education and the fact that many teachers lack ICT skills. Several studies have shown that an important barrier to technology use in schools is simply lack of teacher time to attend training and workshops, and to plan lessons using new materials or methods. Another important factor is the lack of learning technology plans, which engage the whole of a school's teaching staff. Many of the innovation in using learning technologies still rely on individual teachers (…)"   OECD/CERI (1999), p. 58

There is also the need to explore within the learning environment the potential role of a range of professionals other than teachers, whether coming from inside or outside education. New approaches to learning may, beyond the needful revitalisation of teachers themselves, require partnerships with new types of professional having diverse profiles and backgrounds. There may be strategic policy choices to be made between investing principally in the professional development of existing teachers – on the grounds that no serious changes can take place without their close involvement – and in creating new professional roles. For one participant, the issue was one of fairness and effectiveness: how fair is it always to expect teachers to bear the brunt of educational change, including the widespread introduction of ICT? The introduction of a new body of ICT specialists would support the effective adoption of ICT and simultaneously encourage the development of teachers' skills in this area.

There was general agreement on the importance of *intermediaries*, such as brokers or facilitators, in building bridges between the supply and demand for learning. One participant expressed this in terms of having access to persons, including peer-group members, to "help you to learn", which is, in part, to emphasise a community involvement. Several speakers stressed the value of enhancing the role of different community participants, among whom might appear local community "champions", to promote the success of initiatives. Such initiatives could include close attention matched to disadvantaged community groups, including those centred on linguistic and ethnic features. The rapid growth in equipping schools with computers and Internet connectivity has made school access more even, so that digital divide issues related to home access become the more crucial. One way of addressing this concern would be for the enhanced school facilities to be used for extended purposes, such as making special provision for particular community groups.

Linguistic issues are of major policy importance in many countries, given the dominance of the English language in software and the Internet. The desire to promote cultural diversity is one reason behind interest in linguistic issues, but so is the avoidance of social exclusion among non-English-speaking populations. Hence, these matters are critical to various aspects of learning's digital divide. How can they best be addressed? One Roundtable example came from New Zealand, where language – especially Maori – is a prominent feature of political, cultural and educational life. The New Zealand Web portal for teachers is bi-lingual, with the Maori contents presented before the English version. As far as provision for early childhood learning is concerned, there is a Maori ICT network across different centres, characterised by a strong focus on family and inter-generational learning. It would be useful to compile similar examples from other communities and countries.

Further examples might usefully be gathered, concerning initiatives that adopt ICT to address the needs of children and adults with learning difficulties and poor basic skills. As regards literacy education, ICT can prove an effective way of overcoming some of the diffidence and embarrassment experienced by those with basic skills problems (see, in particular, Chapter 6). A project targeted at the Romany community in Hungary has successfully introduced young people to the Internet as a vehicle for communication. It would be interesting to know of other such initiatives, though few would pretend that learning through ICT represents a panacea for those facing the greatest levels of hardship and isolation.

Over and above the discrete elements that contribute to improvement, quality in education is a function of the culture of institutions and whole societies. Schools were criticised by one participant for not acting sufficiently as *service institutions*, while another saw the higher education sector as reluctant to change, more so than primary and secondary schools. Some saw the need for ICT to be used strategically, to help open up new forms of teaching and learning and not just to supplement existing organisational models, since it is only through radical change that the real potential of ICT to enhance learning will be realised. Still more demanding will be the development of new learning models specifically for those who experience different forms of disadvantage – the under-served, the hard and the very hard to reach.

> The model of education that was developed for the industrial age cannot effectively achieve educational empowerment in the information age. With the tools of ICT, we should be able to evolve the conventional model into a new model, moving:
>
> | *from*: | *to*: |
> |---|---|
> | a building | a knowledge infrastructure (print, audio, video, digital) |
> | a student | a learner |
> | a teacher (as provider of knowledge) | a teacher (as a tutor and facilitator) |
>
> It is in this model that the digital divide becomes an educational divide, and bridging it becomes a human need, an educational necessity, and a global urgency (…). We should aggressively explore and innovate; we should cautiously apply; we should fight the shift from education to technology.
>
> *Wadi D. Haddad.*

Although participants stressed repeatedly that the digital divide must be understood in much broader terms than the purely technical, the technological issues should not be ignored. The Roundtable heard of the Swedish goal of giving broad bandwidth access to all and a Canadian initiative to ensure universal connectivity, examples both of policies aimed at widening the access to learning. Reference was also made to the Korean *Edutopia* initiative, which brings together consortia of institutions to provide for lifelong learning on-line. The emerging wireless technologies and digital television have great potential, but the appropriate technology for extending learning across the digital divide will often not be state-of-the-art, and indeed in many circumstances should not be. Imaginative combinations of different media should be examined and evaluated, including traditional television and radio. The Mexican Telesecundaria programme (see Chapter 2) is one such example. Despite the appearance of ever-cheaper technologies, several participants underlined that the cost issue is and will remain critical, especially for poor countries and communities.

DIFFERENT PUBLIC AND PRIVATE SECTOR CONTRIBUTIONS

An important focus for Roundtable discussion was the different roles of government, education systems, communities, and the market. With wide variation in political cultures and traditions, it is impossible to generalise about ideal roles, but it is possible to clarify the questions and issues that need to be addressed, as illustrated by one participant:

> "In a fast moving and complex picture, where the pace of commercial developments constantly extends both the spectrum of knowledge and the scale of possibility, current pressures are to widen rather than to narrow the ICT 'access gap'. Cost issues, especially as between commercial and public service users, will also continue to be difficult. Absolute cost reductions in the market are regularly offset by increases in technological potential. Among the pressing issues needing to be kept under debate are therefore:
> • What is the best model for combining central and local initiative in addressing the needs of particular user communities, and at what level or levels should the initiative be taken (local "ownership" versus area consistency)?

- How far do national and local conditions encourage and facilitate the work of voluntary organisations and agencies in addressing this major agenda, and how are the appropriate operational areas defined?"
- How far should business and commerce go in helping to address socially important but essentially non-commercial goals, and how far can such support be systematised to improve the yield from individually valuable initiatives?
- What are the most appropriate funding models within individual countries, or provinces of large countries, and within less developed economies with many urgent and pressing educational priorities, perhaps at the most basic level?
- What role can international organisations play in addressing access and usage problems that are essentially sub-national and locally determined?
- Can a basic core of networking facilities and capability be identified that can act as a common denominator across education systems in countries at differing economic states of development, such that inter-communication and content exchange can usefully take place?"

Robin Ritzema, U.K. Representative

Within the multiplicity of these relationships, certain participants stressed the need for a powerful lead from government, while others perceived a more detached role in terms of regulating the market. The perceived impact of market forces also varies, one view being that markets always widen inequalities, another that they can be an effective way of identifying new demand. Similarly, there were diverse views concerning the responsibilities of the private sector in relation to the digital divide. Some saw the major commercial interests as accepting a major responsibility, and looking for guidance on how to exercise it, but others were less sanguine. Such viewpoints are not necessarily unresolvable. If the commercial ICT players have hitherto made little impact in poor communities, for instance, there may be scope for a larger role, given an appropriately supportive framework within which this can be achieved. Making this happen, however, is another matter.

New relationships are developing in markets, with changing boundaries. One viewpoint was that the traditional educational publishing industry is entering into terminal decline, as Web-based materials take over. It was suggested that learning provision delivered via the Internet and e-commerce, along with private sector certification of competence, will threaten established practices in education systems, especially at the tertiary level. On the other hand, it was observed that the resilience of existing institutions and arrangements has often been underestimated, and the long-heralded end of schools and textbooks has yet to arrive.

The issue has to be faced as to how public policy can come to terms with market forces. Without an adequate return on investment for producers, high costs will lead to *market failure*. This could imply that without explicit government interventions to lower costs to the individual, many will not be brought into learning. Similar arguments were advanced during the Roundtable concerning poor countries, and the difficulties they have to invest in expensive equipment and infrastructure. Costs are important, but clearly not the only factor for bringing the hard-to-reach into learning. Public-private partnerships are one way to take, as in Germany where an initiative aimed at increasing the use of the Internet by women and older people involves *Deutsche Telecom* and *Brigitte* magazine. Again, however, the question arises of the extent to which such initiatives are successful in getting to those who are the really hard to reach.

In Hungary, the *Soros Foundation*[24] has produced a number of school-level ICT programmes co-ordinated with government policy. Particular emphasis has been given by the Foundation to supporting school activities: developing ICT curricula and teaching materials; building the capacity of school libraries and supporting the further training of teacher-librarians; generally providing support and advice for schools. One of its initiatives, described in the extract below, is aimed squarely at aspects of the digital divide that public policy might otherwise miss. As described in the extract, having developed and implemented this programme, the Foundation then seeks to enter into partnership with the public authorities so that it can be continued and sustained elsewhere.

> *Soros Foundation Small Region Information Technology Programme*
> "As early as 1997, the Ministry of Education launched *Sulinet*, the School Network Programme to connect all high schools and the larger elementary schools to the Internet (…). At the same time, elementary schools in small villages were left out of the central development and were threatened by an increasing gap between the level of facilities they offer [and those in] institutions already included in the School Net Programme.

---

24. See http://www.soros.org/.

This moved the Foundation into launching an ICT educational experiment for small regions, offering four schools rotating use of equipment (...). Under the scheme, the Foundation sought areas of small villages whose schools were poorly supplied with educational information technology facilities, and were prepared and able to co-operate with each other. The groups selected, consisting of four villages, had to make agreements concerning joint computer education. The Foundation provided support for each group in the form of a local area network consisting of 15 multimedia computers to be held in each village for two months at a time. One teacher travels along with the hardware to the four locations, so that one well-qualified information technology teacher is sufficient to teach the students in the four schools. After the first two-month intensive course, when the computers and the teacher leave, a well-equipped computer with Internet access is installed in the school library for the permanent use of the pupils and teachers. This rotating scheme provides the four villages with full, permanent computer education.

In order to get the programme off to a good start, the Foundation centrally arranged and financed the installation of the computers in 12 sites, and provided a training course for every affected school. In 1998, 17 applications were received, of which 6 were awarded grants (65 000 USD). In 1999, 3 new small regions associations joined the programme.

Once the programme is accomplished, the Foundation will offer the model (method, know-how and experience) to the Ministry of Education, local authorities and the International Network of Soros Foundations. It is our intention to develop at least one co-operative model in each county in 2000."

Judit Ronai, Soros Foundation

CONCLUSION – EXCHANGE AND EVALUATION

It is desirable to gain a balanced view of the strengths and weaknesses of the various initiatives, for possible application and development in different circumstances. What are the contributory features within the infrastructure, the organisation, the community? What criteria should be to the fore in evaluating programmes aimed at bridging the digital divide? How can such evaluation best be organised, especially in relation to the non-formal and informal settings of home and community that are far removed from policy reach? There is in fact a general neglect of evaluation in policy implementation. It is also in the nature of high-profile initiatives such as the adoption of ICT to be politically driven, and therefore implemented no matter what evaluation might show. A further constraint regarding ICT in education is the speed of change, which means that decisions are often taken before careful evaluation can be achieved. There is nevertheless a valuable role for research and evaluation, in indicating how the committed resources can best be deployed, and in providing useful pointers for future policy.

A great deal is to be learned from the international exchange of practices that are especially promising or effective in bridging the different dimensions of learning's digital divide. Roundtable participants endorsed the importance of such exchange for highlighting exemplary practice. Even in the absence of in-depth evaluation, there is value in compiling evidence of promising initiatives that use ICT to bring learning to the otherwise disadvantaged. More profound analysis is then needed, however, to establish what exactly is best practice and why it works well.

CHAPTER 8
ICT, Equity and the Challenge
of Lifelong Learning: The Swedish Approach
by
Sten Ljungdahl[25]

INTRODUCTION – THE IMPORTANCE OF EQUITY

Swedish schools are expected to provide education of high quality for all students, regardless of their gender, home district, or social and economic background. This nation-wide commitment to equity is a cornerstone of Swedish education policy. From an international perspective, Sweden has an education system that is homogenous in essential respects, with smaller differences between schools than in many other countries. The performance of schools in different parts of the country is similar. The ablest Swedish students are well matched to corresponding groups in other countries, in terms of both relative quantity and level. In order to make education readily available to every one there are no tuition fees within Swedish state education.

The Swedish government has emphasised lifelong learning as a cornerstone in the struggle for a good society and against unemployment. In addition, the government stresses the necessity to develop skills and knowledge in the workplace,

25. Deputy Director, Ministry of Education and Science, Sweden.

in order to widen employees' opportunities, and ensure the continuing strength of business and industry. A society that invests in education is investing in the future. Investment in education at all levels reduces the risks of exclusion from the employment market and widening of the gaps in society. Increasingly information and communication technology (ICT) is seen as indispensable in giving effect to these aspirations and making education freely available to all.

The *information society* gives the opportunity for a more comprehensive democracy and new forms of civic participation, but at the same time it entails the risks of new gaps opening up within society. School and the other elements in the education system have a key role to play in establishing equitable opportunities for an active participation in social life. The ability to seek and exchange information using data bases and networks is not simply dependent on access to technology, but requires possession of the necessary technical skills. In addition, it calls for basic competence in being able to choose, classify and critically evaluate the information that becomes accessible.

To avoid the emergence of a digital divide, all students must be well acquainted with ICT, able to use it and to benefit from it. An important task is to find ways to compensate for students' disparate capacities and varying access to ICT. At the same time the use of ICT can itself work as a force of change within school, offering new possibilities for presentation of subject content, for working methods and for pedagogy – but only in so far as teachers are empowered to keep up with developments in this field. Knowledge of ICT is a powerful means to develop the individual's capacity for lifelong learning, and generally strengthens people's position in society; it is essential for the future labour market. For Sweden to continue as a successful nation holding its own in the competitive international ICT arena, more technicians and engineers capable of developing the technology of tomorrow are needed.

FORMAL EDUCATION AND THE FOUNDATION FOR LIFELONG LEARNING

A satisfactory standard of basic education for all is the foundation for lifelong learning and an equitable society, beginning with the pre-school. At the age 1-5 years, 73% of all Swedish children participate in pre-school and all six-year olds do so, apart from the 6% already attending compulsory school (Sweden, 1999*a*). The social, environment and pedagogical stimulation that children encounter during their formative years influence their opportunities for later development and learning. Since the urge to learn is already present within a child, the most important task of pre-school and school is to satisfy and sustain this innate curiosity. The national curriculum for pre-school emphasises ICT as a means to promote the communicative and creative abilities of young children.

Compulsory school aims to provide all students with equitable education opportunities that take into account the specific requirements of individuals. Children with differing needs and from different backgrounds come together, but the school has an obligation to allocate special support to those who have difficulty in achieving the goals. It is the task of the school to cater for the varying needs of students, to bridge the gaps in knowledge and to compensate for social disparities. Included in the national curriculum of the compulsory school is the goal that every student shall be able to use ICT as a tool for learning. This means that the education system is required to create good opportunities for teachers and students to benefit from ICT; *digital literacy* is regarded as a basic competence.

Basic education is designed to qualify students in three respects: for life in a democratic society, for an evolving working life and for further learning. It must provide good preparation for all citizens to gain employment and participate in social life, with a broad base of skills and knowledge and a readiness to develop further. No one should leave school without such preparation, since compensating for educational deficiencies later in life is costly, in both human and economic terms. In order to ensure such a preparation for all, there is continuous attention to effecting improvements in the quality of education in every school form and level. Particular efforts are also made to reduce the percentage of students who drop out of school.

Since the beginning of the 1980s *upper secondary education for all* has been a political objective. The present Swedish upper secondary school was fully implemented in the school year 1994/95, in a reform that extended all upper secondary programmes, including vocational, to three years (Sweden, 1991). Entrance requirements for all upper secondary courses were introduced in the school year 1998/99. By means of eight core-subject courses, one third of the content is the same for the programme of every student, thus allowing any course to provide general eligibility for university and college entrance, whilst those who go directly from upper secondary school to employment have a solid foundation for continued learning.

It is the young people themselves who choose which courses to follow, in line with their interests and perceptions of employment market requirements. This has been found to be more effective than central forecasting and direction.

That 98% of the students in each annual cohort proceed to upper secondary school can be seen as an endorsement of the choices on offer – both academic and vocational – and the commitment of schools and municipalities to devising arrangements capable of meeting every student's needs, but it is clearly also a reflection of the labour market situation (Sweden, 1999c).

Since the early 1980s, municipalities have carried additional responsibilities for those young people aged 16-18, who did not proceed to upper secondary and are unemployed. Appropriate programmes of study, vocational orientation and support, have been devised to match each individual's needs. Under the Education Act of 1985, municipalities are obliged to offer upper secondary education to all young people up to 20 years old, so long as they have achieved elementary school pass marks in Swedish (or Swedish as a second language), English and mathematics. In 1998 the municipalities also assumed follow-up responsibility for unemployed young people aged 20-24. The responsibility begins if employment, education or a suitable labour market initiative cannot be provided, within 90 days of the young person registering as an employment seeker.

For students not qualified to begin upper secondary courses – 10% of those who finished compulsory school in 1999 (Sweden, 1999b) – individual programmes are available to help them compensate for their lack of knowledge and skills. More than half the students who began such individual programme in 1994, immediately after compulsory school, had left the upper secondary school one or two years later. However, after one year 35% transferred to a full upper secondary course, and of these half successfully completed it three years later (Sweden, 1999c).

ICT IN SCHOOLS

The strategies to spread the use of ICT in education are entering a new development phase. Thus far, resources have been spent on the technical infrastructure, but the focus must increasingly be on learning and not merely on the technology itself. The intention must be to take advantage of the new opportunities which ICT affords to promote quality learning processes: it enables schools to develop the learning environment in ways that give students a more active role, that support the ability to find information and transform it into knowledge.

A national action plan

Schools must provide access to ICT for all students and develop their capacity to use it, and all students should have gained familiarity with ICT by the time they leave school. In Spring 1998, the Swedish parliament adopted an action plan for ICT in schools (Sweden, 1998a), covering pre-school, compulsory school, special school, Sami (minority ethnic group) school and upper secondary school. During the three-year period 1999-2001, the government is investing 1.5 billion SEK to promote school use of ICT as a pedagogical tool, and to expand the horizons of the classroom.

The action plan included the formation of a *Delegation for ICT in Schools*,[26] charged with ensuring its implementation. More specifically, the delegation is to:

- Distribute state grants to the municipalities to improve the Internet access of their schools.
- Create opportunities for all students and teachers to have e-mail addresses.
- Offer in-service training activities for about 60 000 teachers in teams (40% of the total number of teachers).
- Make computers available for home use by teachers who have obtained an ICT certificate.
- Support the development of the Swedish Schoolnet and the European Schoolnet.
- Make special arrangements for functionally disabled students (see below).

Access to computers by teachers and students is one of the most important prerequisites for the development of computer use at school. Since 1993, the Swedish National Agency for Education (*Skolverket*) has made regular surveys of the distribution of computers within the Swedish school system. The latest survey (Sweden, 1999d) showed 10 students per computer in the compulsory school, five in upper secondary school and nine in adult education; 85% of municipal compulsory schools are connected to the Internet, and 95% of municipal upper secondary schools.

ICT for students with functional disabilities

In less than a decade, ICT has entirely revolutionised the educational situation of many children and young people with functional disabilities. According to

---

26. The *Delegation for ICT in Schools* is a temporary body responsible to the Swedish National Agency for Special Needs Education (SIH), an advisory and support body that also produces special teaching materials.

the Swedish National Agency for Special Needs Education (SIH), there is now a computer as a personal and educational aid for every student with gravely impaired vision, and the same provision for children with severe motor disabilities. In the 1990s, special schools emerged as one of the educational environments with the highest computer density, with statutory schools for the intellectually handicapped having in 1999 an average of one computer per four students.

Offering disabled children and youth a quality education requires special competence on the part of teachers and specially-adapted educational materials. Since individual municipalities cannot readily meet these needs, SIH has been charged with facilitating the schooling of students with disabilities, and offers special pedagogical support without charge, to both state and independent schools. SIH has a well-developed expertise concerning how to ensure accessibility to ICT for disabled students and what is appropriate software for students with special needs. It offers design guidelines for educational software and instructional support for putting materials on the Internet. It gives economic support for the development of learning media for handicapped students, such as teaching media in sign language for students with impaired hearing, in order to develop their knowledge of sign language, Swedish and mathematics. Training of tutors for the intellectually handicapped is offered at regional level by an expert panel, leading to opportunities for in-service training of teachers at local level in the state system.

Teachers and headteachers

An important precondition for development in schools is sound educational leadership. Since the decentralisation of the official Swedish school system in the beginning of the 1990s, the leadership responsibility of the headteacher has increased. Much therefore depends on whether the school head is convinced that the quality of teaching and learning can be raised by the use of ICT as an everyday teaching tool. Because the level of ICT development in schools is so largely dependent on the management, the government has introduced special measures for management training.

Another important factor for the adoption of ICT in schools is that teachers must be familiar with the technology and how it can be used most effectively to promote the desired pedagogical objectives. Unless teachers are so equipped, ICT will not be used effectively by schools, nor will it be able to contribute to the development of schools as centres of learning. Mindful of this, the government has decided that ICT must be a major feature of teacher training, so that everyone who qualifies as a teacher will have knowledge of the educational potential of ICT and personal experience of using it. According to a survey made by the Delegation for ICT in Schools, Autumn 1999, nearly 50% of Swedish teachers have participated in one or more courses in computer use, and 10-15% have completed a pedagogically-oriented course.

The Swedish schoolnet

In 1992, the National Agency for Education was commissioned by the government to promote the development and implementation of the national ICT policy within the school sector, by developing a national schoolnet and building up a network resource centre. The Swedish schoolnet is a computer network for schools, the contents of which include quality-assured links (portals) organised according to teaching subjects, meeting places and a notice board for sharing ideas and information, and a register of school e-mail addresses. The *Multimedia Bureau*, run by the National Agency for Education, is available as part of the schoolnet and serves as a source of materials, ideas, courses and information. The Bureau is also intended for use as a tool for distance publishing and to facilitate exchange of experience. Its overall aim is to stimulate school use of the new media by teachers and students.

The European Schoolnet (EUN), established through a Swedish initiative and working in co-operation with the European Commission, is a network of national and other schoolnets available for schools, teachers, students and the public. It promotes co-operation between schools in respect of pedagogical issues, in order to stimulate the effective use of ICT in European schools.

THE ADULT POPULATION

Differences in computer use in Sweden

The distribution of computers in Swedish homes is very uneven. More than half of those who have completed tertiary education have access to a computer, compared with only a third of those with no more than statutory education. Far fewer wage earners than salaried employees and graduates have personal computers at home, perhaps because they are less-well paid and cannot afford the investment (Sweden, 1999e). In order to stimulate the use of ICT, trade unions offer their members low-priced computer packages, which are also offered by employers against pay deductions. Thus many more people in various groups will be able to have a computer to use at home. Use is growing rapidly – in 1998, 68% of the population (aged 15-84 years) had access to a computer and Internet in their homes; compared with 58% in 1996 (Sweden, 1998*b*).

A study on the use of the Internet among the Swedish population, based on figures up to and including 1996, shows marked differences between various population groups. Internet use in big city areas was three times that in the countryside. Young people were more likely to be users than older people. Men are much more frequent users than women, with the differences between men and women being greater among younger people. Those with a university education use the Internet much more than people with a lower level of education.

Schools as community centres

Many people lack access to a computer. With the Internet growing in importance as a communication medium, those who do not themselves have access to it will be at an increasing disadvantage. Furthermore, most households with Internet access have a slow modem connection, whereas Sweden's schools are becoming equipped by the government with very powerful Internet connections, that permits new areas of use such as transmission of video. It would be advantageous for these school facilities to be made accessible to the community outside school hours.

The government therefore sees interesting scope for the use of school premises and equipment after the end of the school day. However, using the Internet to advantage requires not only the right equipment, but the necessary skills for achieving the connection, *i.e.* knowing how to find interesting, relevant and reliable information, and how to work with it. Given the right organisation, it should be possible to keep the premises open and provide qualified help to those who are interested in using the school equipment. In addition, if the schools are connected to the Internet via a municipal network, the high-speed connection can be used outside school hours from other premises connected to the same network. Schools can thus become well-equipped resource-centres for the various adult education schemes and for the activities of other associations and societies. Closer collaboration between schools and other institutions might also be realised – such as employment training and computer centres – making schools the natural local centres for flourishing community networks.

Higher and adult education

Universities have a key role in the investment in knowledge and education. They are responsible for practically the whole of higher education in Sweden.

The government has given priority to expanding higher education, both to give more young people places and to extend opportunities to adults. The objective is that all qualified applicants should be offered places in higher education, which should be available at universities nation-wide.

Increasing numbers are applying for admission to higher education, so that the student total has increased by just over 80% in the last decade, and is expected to be approximately 300 000 in the year 2000 (Sweden, 1999a). It is seen as particularly important to boost recruitment from groups that have not traditionally experienced higher education. Since 1977 any person is eligible who has reached the age of 25, has the skills in Swedish and English equivalent to upper secondary level, and has been employed for at least four years. Those who have completed upper secondary school, but lack the subject background for the university studies they want, are offered a basic induction year, whether within adult education or at university. Usually this year is used to compensate for low levels in mathematics and science, but for immigrant students it is more likely to be in language and cultural skills.

A typical feature of Swedish education is the opportunity to return later in life to complete compulsory and upper secondary education. The Swedish system of municipal adult education offers an infrastructure for lifelong learning that enables people to satisfy their need to advance their knowledge and personal development, with opportunities for switching between study and work throughout adult life. In July 1995 computer centres run by municipalities were introduced as a supplement to the regular labour market training, with the aim of giving opportunity for the unemployed to become proficient with ICT and to be stimulated to further study. In 1997 a five-year programme of investment and development in adult education was initiated by the Swedish government and municipalities (Sweden, 1996). The major objective is to up-date labour market and education policy, as an important element in the government's bid to halve unemployment by the year 2000.

The primary target group of the new adult education initiative is unemployed adults who lack the full upper secondary education, but it is also aimed at employees who left statutory school early. The programme helps participants to achieve the necessary qualifications and competence levels for study at a higher level, and strengthens the foundations for lifelong learning. Municipal authorities that are charged with implementing this initiative apply for state funding, which is provided for a total of 100 000 full-time students per year, of whom 67% are women. Funding is allocated in proportion to the number of unemployed people in the municipality who have a low level of education. Computer science is the subject most frequently sought within the initiative, accounting for about 16% in national courses at upper secondary level and 33% in local courses (Sweden, 2000).

There are two national schools for adults, within which the government has initiated the development of flexible ICT-supported open and distance learning. These two schools are delivering programmes partly or wholly by distance learning, for which they are becoming development centres. On 1 July 1999 a new authority for distance education (Distum) was established in Härnösand (Sweden, 1998*c*).

Adult education is also available outside the public system, within eleven nation-wide voluntary education associations, which operate some 150 private adult residential colleges known as *Folk High Schools* (Sweden, 1998*d*). The overall aim of this popular adult education movement is to reinforce opportunities for people to affect their own living conditions. The colleges offer alternative educational possibilities for those over 18 years old (sometimes 16), enabling them to work to the competence levels of compulsory and upper secondary school. These voluntary associations provide a wide range of different study circles in the use of computers and common software applications, some of which are for specific groups such as retired people or women.

A pilot scheme, one-third operated and financed by trade and industry, is offering to 12 000 full-time students vocational education qualifications at post-secondary level, that are designed to be the equivalent of upper secondary education. The educational programmes are organised in close co-operation with local and regional working life and include work experience. In its final report, presented towards the end of 1999, the responsible committee for advanced vocational education recommended that the scheme should become permanent (Sweden, 1999*f*).

Women and ICT

At the heart of the just society is equity between men and women. More women are needed as active participants in this technological world, both to meet the demand for extra personnel – the number of people engaged in ICT is rising rapidly – and because women can help to adapt the technology to people's real needs and ways of functioning. It will, however, require a culture change in ICT for women to be given access to technology on their own terms. Whilst this is increasingly necessary for economic well-being, it is more fundamentally what an equitable society demands.

In public debate, it is often observed that ICT was created by and for men. For the pioneers in the industry, love of the technology was central, and became an end in itself. The notion of user-friendliness was unknown. Conversely, women appear less likely to be interested in the technology for its own sake, but are more concerned with the benefits it may afford. The proportion of women on computer-oriented courses in higher education is consistently less than 10%, and in the computer industry women make up a small minority. There is for ICT a correlation similar to that between gender and the natural sciences: girls are interested in seeing context and meaning, whereas boys more often see technology as having intrinsic value. Swedish society has to avoid men becoming in consequence the winners in the information society (Sweden, 1998e).

Several things are needed if girls are to be given better scope for using and learning about ICT. One is that teachers must be better aware of the difference in girls' and boys' use of ICT, and work actively to give both sexes equal opportunities. The learning environment must be arranged in such a way as to appeal to girls, giving them equal access to equipment and ample opportunities to pursue their own interests independent of boys.

CONCLUSION

ICT has become a natural part of people's everyday life, whether at work or in society at large. The number of people using computers in Sweden rose from one third of the population in 1985 to two thirds in 1995, and ICT is gaining ground in virtually every workplace, where in consequence working life has been dramatically transformed. Whilst these developments generate new opportunities within society, they also impose new challenges, especially for education. The new technology will not replace teachers, textbooks or the classroom, but make the tasks of the teacher more stimulating and at the same time more demanding, since teachers must learn to master ICT as a professional and pedagogical tool. It will create new combinations of opportunities to promote learning, and transform the relationships between teachers and students.

Alongside the pervasive appearance of ICT – and supported by it – lifelong learning has become a reality in working and social life. Completed formal education leads naturally to further development and up-dating of knowledge and experience, both inside and outside the workplace. The responsibility for this is shared between the individual and the employer, but the driving force rests within the individual human being, who must be self-confident and motivated by the urge to acquire new knowledge. Those leaving school and entering society must be equipped to relearn, to learn what is new, and to learn more – on a lifelong basis.

CHAPTER 9
Other National Approaches
Portugal, the United Kingdom, Japan,
the United States, Finland

by
**João Santos, Robin Ritzema, Takashi Sakamoto, Robert Muller,
Jouni Kangasniemi[27]**

This chapter is drawn from those national statements of educational ICT policy that were distributed at the Roundtable, excluding Sweden which is the subject of the previous chapter. It indicates how such policies are generally designed to be inclusive, and relates particular efforts to tackle the digital divide through education.

PORTUGAL

The priorities

In its programme for 1999-2003 (Portugal, 2000*a*), the government presented the challenge of building the information and knowledge society as

---

27. João Santos, Chef de Cabinet to the Secretary of Education, Portugal; Robin Ritzema, International Educational Consultant, United Kingdom; Takashi Sakamoto, Director-General, National Institute of Multimedia Education, Japan; Robert Muller, Deputy Assistant Secretary, U.S. Department of Education; Jouni Kangasniemi, Project Manager, Higher Education Evaluation Council, Finland.

one of two top priorities, the other being to promote equal opportunities for men and women. Four areas are identified for attention, the first being to promote access to the Internet, by quadrupling over the next few years the number of personal computers so connected and stimulating the "family market". Public facilities will be created by local administrations to provide Internet access, and within the next three years up to a million e-mail addresses will be supplied, free of charge. Portuguese content on the Internet will be expanded dramatically, being at present only 1% of the English content.

Secondly, the government aims to expand the Science, Technology and Society Network,[28] to reach all schools. This will affect the first cycle of basic education (grades 1-4), since schools from grades 5-12 and municipal libraries are already connected. The third aim is to implement a national programme of training and certification in basic ICT skills for all citizens. For the school population, this might be linked in the near future to the leaving certificate at the end of compulsory education (grade 9 at age 15). Finally, the public authorities will increasingly offer access via the Internet to all the information which they make available.

In their formal education, all children should experience access to ICT, which requires improving the availability of suitable educational software and Internet products in Portuguese, and a better student/computer ratio. Within the national curriculum, there has been an enhancement of project work, in respect of both technological and civic education, with dedicated curricular time provided (Portugal, 1998). Attention will also be given to adult education and training courses with an integral ICT component, including courses at a distance, whether for those who do not possess basic literacy and numeracy or those seeking to improve existing skills. The recently-created National Agency for Adult Education and Training[29] will play a major role. In addition, it is intended to extend the educational use of ICT to Portuguese-speaking countries and Portuguese citizens living abroad.

There are several specific strategies in pursuit of these different aims, as is discussed below. Technical support will be provided for all teachers, by means of school-based in-service training, and active partnerships with universities and colleges of education. Innovative teaching strategies in the educational use of ICT will be developed and examples of good practice disseminated on a national

---

28. Rede Ciencia, Tecnologia e Sociedade.

29. Agencia Nacional de Educaçao e Formaçao de Adultos.

scale. The Third Programme for the Development of Education in Portugal,[30] submitted in 1999 to the European Commission, provides for around 100 000 computers for basic and secondary schools by the year 2006, to bring the student/computer ratio down to 10:1. Alongside this, the Ministry of Education will validate 200 different multimedia products across a wide range of subjects, from which 250 000 copies will be purchased for distribution (Portugal, 2000*b*). A Green Paper on the Information Society (Portugal, 1997) established the national strategy for the dissemination of ICT, and stressed as a major priority the need to combat *info-exclusion*.

The opportunities for statutory education need to be enlarged, to provide pre-school and compulsory schooling up to grade 9 for all, and ultimately universal secondary education or post-compulsory education and training to 18 years of age. There is need of a national curriculum that ensures attention to the fundamental intellectual tools – Portuguese, mathematics, experimental sciences – as well as the development of other high-level content and skills, including history, the arts and technological literacy. Young people should be able to enjoy the opportunities of the information and knowledge society in an open, critical and creative way, without a widening gap between the *haves* and the *have-nots* and a growing structural *underclass*. There is an urgent need also to upgrade the educational skills of the large majority of the adult population.[31] All such changes should be aimed towards creating a more democratic and participatory society.

Within the European Strategy for Employment, the Portuguese government stresses the importance of enhancing the employability of the labour force, whether through active employment policies or wider training opportunities for poorly-skilled workers who left school prematurely. Common elements of the training include improved practical use of Portuguese and mathematics, learning a foreign language, and technological literacy. The target groups up to 2006 are workers aged 18 to 42 years who did not attend school for longer than 9 years (nearly 2 million being in this category), and those aged 43 to 52 years with no more than 4 years of schooling (around half a million) (Portugal, 2000*b*).

---

30. Programa de Desenvolvimento da Educaçao em Portugal, PRODEP III.
31. Some ten years ago, 74% of Portuguese citizens between the ages of 15 and 64 had no more than 6 years of schooling. In 1995, the national literacy study co-ordinator revealed that 70% of the active population was unable to perform more than very elementary tasks related to reading, writing and arithmetic (Portugal, 1996).

As in other countries and regions, inequalities arise between different social, economic and educational backgrounds. They threaten social cohesion and diminish the freedom and self-esteem of individuals. Although ICT may add greatly to existing inequalities, it expands the capacity to reduce them when used in a visionary way. Thus the notion of equitable access to the new technologies is of paramount concern. It is envisaged that technological literacy for all will be attainable through the interaction of schools, industry, central, regional and local administration, families and other groups, helped by the state. The state can provide the infrastructure, such as information highways, science and technology networks, school equipment and *Digital Cities*; it can offer tax concessions for the private purchase of computers and software. Furthermore, the state can promote the development of a dynamic ICT industry, for instance by legislation to facilitate the expansion of electronic trade or to protect copyright.

ICT in the school system

Since the launching of the first national ICT project, the extent of change has been enormous. Mobile phones, satellite and cable TV, and PCs have become commonplace. Computer technology has evolved quickly, so that the advanced expertise required in the 1980s to deal with even mundane aspects of computers is no longer an obstacle for the novice. Hence, the nature of the educational challenges is also changing rapidly. Basic ICT literacy is now readily acquired informally, allowing attention to turn to the didactic and pedagogical issues relating to the use of information technologies, as well as their applications in the administrative modernisation of schools. Computers no longer represent just a subject to be learned, but provide everyday instruments for teaching, learning and working.

Created in 1996, the NONIO *Twenty-first Century Programme*[32] was designed with a four-year life-span. It is concerned with the application and development of ICT, training in its use, the creation and development of educational software, the dissemination of information and international co-operation. Support for the projects in schools is provided by expertise centres – universities, colleges of education, in-service teacher-training centres, and teachers' associations. More than 700 different school projects are involved, with national competitions to promote the development of educational software and support materials.

32. Programa NONIO-Seculo XXI; see http://www.dapp.min-edu.pt/nonio/nonio.htm.

Since 1994, the Ministry of Education network has connected the central and regional networks of educational administration, enabling access to the Internet, Intranet, e-mail service, and video conferencing.[33] At present, this network is being expanded to the regional branches of the Education Inspectorate and to the national teacher training programme. The *Internet in Schools* programme of the Ministry of Science and Technology provided (as of September 1999), multimedia computers and Internet connection to almost 2 000 public and private schools, 80 cultural, scientific and educational associations, 250 public libraries and 15 museums. The next step will be to extend this to about 8 000 primary schools (grades 1-4) and to the 150 teacher-training centres (Portugal, 1997).

The *Good Hope Programme*[34] was created in 1998, with defined domains in which to identify good practice for dissemination. It aims to promote quality learning for all, to improve school organisation, to increase school-community interaction, and to extend the educational use of ICT. There are 29 projects in schools of all levels throughout the country, four of which are focused on ICT. One of the four (primary), is linked to transnational partners in the United States (Hartford University), Brazil and Spain, with an emphasis on environmental issues. Another (secondary), is focused on learning Portuguese, and involves all Portuguese-speaking countries. A third is aimed at improving general technological skills and scientific thinking across all subjects.

UNITED KINGDOM

Britain, with other developed and developing countries, is moving rapidly towards the integration of new technology across all levels of education, building on more than twenty years' experience from the earliest educational computing. The need to study with, and through, new technology is embedded in all subjects of the national curriculum. Networking of learning materials is developing rapidly in schools and at the post-school level, including vocational training. Universities were the first public institutions in the United Kingdom to use high bandwidth connections for data exchange and teaching, which is surely the direction for the future. There are government initiatives for national technology-backed learning

---

33. Rede de Informaçao e Comunicaçao do Ministerio do Educaçao – RICOME; see http://www.dapp.min-edu.pt.

34. *Programa Boa Esperança*; see http://www.iie.min-edu.pt/proj/boa-esperanca/index.htm.

---

programmes, and many other innovative strategies at the local and community levels.

Britain's *National Grid for Learning*[35] already incorporates a web site of quality-controlled and indexed learning materials for professionals, with materials for students to follow. It offers a starting point for learning quests of all kinds, with access to materials, courses, professional contacts and links with learning networks in the United Kingdom and elsewhere. All school teachers, post-school lecturers and trainers are being equipped to use the new technologies within their subject specialisms, which goes well beyond training in ICT skills *per se*, and which will stimulate use of the National Grid. The target is for all schools, colleges, libraries and museums to be networked early in the decade. Through devolved provincial and local implementation, there is massive scope for innovation by individuals and institutions. Progress is encouraging and well on course.

The *University for Industry*[36] (UfI) to be launched nationally in Autumn 2000, will target new and existing post-school learners, and engage them in the process of lifelong learning. Development centres are already operating in 68 locations, with 1 000 expected by March 2001. The *Learndirect* telephone helpline operated by UfI provides free information and advice about learning and careers, with a database of learning opportunities available from Spring 2000. Opportunities will expand markedly for study in homes and workplaces, as well as in learning centres, as new products are commissioned to fill existing and emerging skill needs. UfI will start with around 60% of their learning products delivered through web technology, a figure set to rise steadily in the following years. The initial focus will be on the areas of basic skills, small and medium-sized businesses, and ICT. Through its promotion of lifelong learning, the initiative will contribute directly to both personal and economic development.

From September 2000, around 700 of the *ICT Learning Centres*[37] will also help bridge the gap between those who have ready access to ICT and those who do not, aiming to give more people more opportunities to engage in society and improve their own situations. By developing their learning in such ways, people will gain in confidence and have a better chance of getting and keeping a job. Local organisations will have access to funding to set up innovative projects

---

35. See http://www.ngfl.gov.uk.

36. See http://www.ufiltd.co.uk.

37. See http://www.dfee.gov.uk/ict-learning-centres/int.htm.

aimed at local needs. Centres will be flexible in their approach, varying in scale from a small PC-based facility in a village hall or mobile project on a bus, to a state-of-the-art centre in a shopping mall. Through *recycled computer* schemes – using equipment that meets prescribed standards – access to network learning will be extended to those whose economic circumstances would otherwise make this difficult or impossible.

New directions

Reflecting the high political importance of social inclusion as new technology use expands across society, a multi-disciplinary task force reported to government at the end of 1999 (UK, 2000; see also UK, 1998*a*, 1998*b*) on additional measures that might be taken. Particular emphasis is placed on:

- Strengthening coherence between the present multiplicity of objectives at national and local levels.
- Collaboration between central and local organisations, community and voluntary sectors, and business, to improve access to ICT in deprived neighbourhoods, by providing the technical infrastructure, applications relevant to the interests of the groups in question, and a strategy for longer term sustainability.
- Recognition of the synergy between ICT literacy goals and general literacy goals, the two being mutually supportive.
- Support for "local champions" to engage local people enthusiastically and drive activities forward.
- Setting realistic targets for future technology penetration and usage, following research and analysis.
- Improved networking to spread good practice, especially in relation to specific social groups.
- Recognition that costs are and will remain significant – hence, for example, continuing dialogue with telecommunications providers to ensure access to ICT for those in difficult economic circumstances.

JAPAN

Promoting the advanced information and communication society

Today's society has entered an *information revolution*, comparable in scale with the civil and industrial revolutions of the 18th and 19th centuries. In 1995, the Office for the Promotion of the Advanced Information and Communication

Society, an organisation headed by the Prime Minister of Japan, defined today's society as:

> "A society based on a new socio-economic system that realises the unrestricted creation, distribution, and sharing of information and knowledge produced from human intellectual activity; and that harmonises the life, culture, industry, economy, nature, and environment as a whole".

Education is naturally part of this system

In response, the Ministry of Education, Science, Sports and Culture (Monbusho) defined guidelines for action, as did other ministries (Japan, 1995). The guidelines included provision for advanced information and communications networks, satellite communications, the development of educational methods using these infrastructures, and training programmes for teachers. In the following year, an influential report from the fifteenth Central Council for Education emphasised the need to address educational problems through a much closer focus on actual circumstances, and to foster the development of children as future leaders in society (Japan, 1996). The report argues that children and society as a whole need *yutori* (room to grow), and therefore proposed a reduction in what is now taught, though with care to maintain the fundamentals.

The report gave a strong and timely focus on technology education. In elementary schools children should become familiar with computers to enrich their learning activities, in part through a *period of integrated study*. Students in junior high schools should develop their computer literacy; and according to their interests be able to learn more advanced computer techniques. In senior high schools, a more active use of computers should be encouraged in each subject, and information-related subjects should be promoted. At all levels, children must understand that the virtual experience offered by technology is no more than a support, whilst real life, society, and nature form the underlying realities.

The third version of the Educational Reform Programme issued by Monbusho in April 1998 reinforced these directions for change. It called for the systematic provision of information and communication networks in schools, and the installation of education centres as cores of wide networks linking schools. Teacher education required a training curriculum and continuing staff development in technological literacy. In addition, The July 1998 report of the Curriculum Council recommended the more active use of ICT in all subjects across all school levels:

- Better use of ICT in the *period of integrated study* and each subject in primary schools.
- Compulsory informatics units in middle-school home economics and technical subjects, such as practical skills for basic computer use.
- The establishment of a new compulsory informatics subject in high school.

In line with the recommendation of the Curriculum Council, the New Standard Course of Study was issued in December 1998. The active use of ICT in the *period of integrated study* was especially emphasised, and related to international understanding, the environment, information technology and social welfare.

More recently still, in July 1999, the Japanese government set up the *Virtual Agency* (Japan, 1999), an inter-departmental government task force directly responsible to the Prime Minister. The Virtual Agency brings together Monbusho, the Ministry of International Trade and Industry, the Ministry of Post and Telecommunication, and the Ministry of Local Affairs. It has identified the need for change as a key challenge for Japanese education, whether for children, teachers, or schools. In terms of strategies, the Virtual Agency has proposed the following agenda to be accomplished by 2005:

- Provide computers and Internet access in every classroom in all schools.
- Ensure high-speed Internet access in all schools.
- Equip every teacher to be able to teach using ICT.
- Support information technology use in schools via personnel from local districts and industries.
- Promote the development and delivery of high quality education via collaboration between governmental agencies and industry.
- Establish a National Centre for Educational Information.

The promotion of ICT in education can no longer be regarded as an issue for cultural and educational policies only; it is a national priority. There is growing recognition that it is inextricably related to the issue of a country's survival in the 21st century. It calls for the revision of curriculum standards, along with the provision of hardware and software and Internet access for all schools and students.

Educational use of ICT

As of March 1999, the Internet was used in around 27% of elementary schools, 43% of junior high schools, and 64% of senior high schools. Monbusho plans to provide Internet access to all schools by 2001. Two so-called *100-School Networking Projects* have completed their two-year programmes since the first was launched in 1994, focusing on activities such as gathering and exchanging information, collaborative learning, and research and network conferencing. Now the *E-square Project*[38] is in progress, to involve all 40 000 schools and expand their use of ICT. Furthermore, the *KonetPlan*[39] has been launched, to link 1 014 schools via the Internet and a video-conferencing system; it embraces activities such as e-mail, information gathering, and homepage creation.

According to a *KonetPlan* survey in May 1998, only 12% of Internet-connected schools had 20 or more such terminals. The Internet was most actively used in elementary schools for social studies, science, and special activities, and in junior high schools for home economics, technology, social studies, and science, with slightly less than four hours' use per week on average. Homepage creation – in nearly two-thirds of the schools – was concerned with such matters as publicity for the school or local community: events, club activities, and students' associations. The main perceived changes for participating students were upgraded computer skills and access to large amounts of information, and for teachers enhanced knowledge of multimedia and use of the Internet for information gathering. Within the *KonetPlan* schools, the video-conferencing system is used more frequently than e-mail, except in senior high schools, which also use CU-SeeMe[40] to a significant extent:

	Elementary	Junior high	Senior high
Videoconferencing	66%	43%	27%
E-mail	53%	41%	40%
CU-SeeMe	1%	3%	17%

As part of a study into the use of advanced information and communications facilities for schools in rural areas, Monbusho has linked schools in these areas with others in urban areas, via optical and digital communications networks

---

38. A school network support project of the Centre for Educational Computing, sponsored by Monbusho, designed also to provide advanced ICT applications; the name comes from a play on *e* for educational and *e* for electronic; see http://www.cec.or.jp.

39. A private-sector project.

40. CU-SeeMe – an audio-visual telephone link between two or more people.

and satellite. The rural children are expected to be stimulated by their urban counterparts, while themselves providing information on their rich natural environment and traditional culture. A supplementary budget provision in 1998 included a plan to connect 118 schools by optical communications: two each from 47 prefectures and 12 cities chosen by the government.

In September 1999, an Advanced Educational Network Model Project was launched in 1 076 schools across 30 local districts nation-wide, using digital subscriber lines, wireless local loops, optical fibre, interactive cable television links, and satellite Internet, along with an *El-Net System* for teacher education and lifelong education. The National Education Centre provides a HUB station serving 20 prefectoral education centres, with a VSAT[41] for the exchange of lectures, seminars and video programmes, which are transmitted to 21 prefectoral lifelong learning centres, 974 libraries and community learning centres, and 119 schools.

UNITED STATES

Bridging the skills gap

There are many current initiatives related to technology and access; this section highlights some of the most prominent recent examples that address different facets of the digital divide. In *schools*, concern about the digital divide led to President Clinton's Technology Literacy Challenge,[42] with four key objectives:

- Modern computers and learning devices to be accessible to every student.
- Classrooms to be connected to one another and to the outside world.
- Educational software to be an integral part of the curriculum, and as engaging as the best video game.
- Teachers to be ready to use and teach with technology.

The challenge led to the creation of a package of federal investments, including $2 billion over five years to put technology in schools, and discounted telecommunications services through the universal service fund. Many educational institutions have become "wired".

---

41. Very Small Aperture Terminal.
42. See http://www.whitehouse.gov/WH/EOP/OP/edtech/challenge.html.

For communities, despite progress in addressing inequities in schools, there is growing concern about lack of access to computers and the Internet for adults and children in their homes and communities. Diverse federal investments, including the Department's new Community Technology Centers Programme,[43] have led to a dramatic surge in the numbers connected to the nation's information infrastructure. In its first year, 750 applications were received for 40 grants (totalling $10 million) to establish or expand community technology centres in low-income rural and urban neighbourhoods. An additional $32.5 million has been appropriated for the financial year 2000, which will support over 350 new and expanded centres.

As regards *family literacy,* the America Reads Challenge[44] – reading independently by the end of the third grade – is focusing attention nationally on fostering reading skills, and on promoting family literacy through distance education and technology. The Family Literacy Project is the third segment in a video-and-print series begun by Crossroads Café, targeted to those learning English. This series will produce 18 videos for TV broadcast, to be used in a literacy programme or at home by adult learners.

Anytime, anywhere: The Learning Anytime Anywhere Partnerships[45] include colleges, universities, businesses, community organisations, or other entities to deliver quality post-secondary distance education.

The economic case: The Conference Board report *Turning Skills into Profit* (Bloom and Lafleur, 1999) examines the economic benefits of workplace education programmes. Interviews were conducted with employers, employees, and union representatives from over 40 private and public sector workplaces throughout the United States. This report highlights the many economic benefits of workplace education programmes – to companies, employees and the wider community – and will be widely distributed. Additionally, a workplace education benefits tool kit will be developed and a national conference held to promote literacy in the workplace.

Many other efforts are underway to help citizens access and use technology more effectively to reach their learning objectives. Whether through high school

---

43. See http://www.ed.gov.offices/OVAE/CTC/index.html.

44. In 1997, President Clinton asked Americans to come together to ensure all children read well. See http://www.ed.gov/inits/americareads.

45. See http://www.ed.gov/offices/OPE/FIPSE/LAAP.

reform efforts, school-to-work programmes, or the increased focus on contextual teaching and learning and teacher development, the integration of technology into educational practice is at the fore of the government agenda.

Policy and implementation challenges

At the federal level, current provision for adult basic education, secondary education and English-as-a-Second-Language programmes is small compared with national need. Current federal support is estimated at 6-8% of total government expenditure in this field – not large, but with the potential to make a major impact. In an important national initiative,[46] Vice President Gore brought together key leaders from business, organised labour, education, and all levels of government, to synthesise current thinking on promising practices in workforce learning. Recommendations and commitments from the group cover several broad areas:

- New partnerships and collaborations should be initiated among traditional and non-traditional partners, from which a host of workforce development efforts can be launched. This was the group's overarching recommendation, in spite of knowing it is hard to achieve.
- There should be delivery of education, training, and learning tied to high standards, that leads to useful credentials and meets labour market needs. High expectations and standards for all learners was the second major focus of the group's recommendations.
- Improved access to financial resources for lifetime learning is needed for all citizens, including those in low-wage jobs. Too often, students, employees and employers are not aware of the full range of tools and services available to them.
- Learning should be promoted at a time and place and in a manner – anytime, anywhere – that meets workers' needs.
- Awareness and motivation to participate in education, training, and learning should be stimulated. The group focused on the need to develop a culture of lifelong learning, where people better understand the benefits of investing in education and training.

Each major recommendation was accompanied by action steps and specific commitments by group members, to further lifelong learning for all citizens,

---

46. The Vice President's 21st Century Skills Leadership Group; see: www.vpskillssummit.org.

not just those on the *have* side of the digital divide. Those in government must place a premium on innovation and creativity, on challenging conventional wisdom and traditional ways of operating; they need to be entrepreneurs, embracing change as a way of life, and finding ways for everyone to benefit from the information revolution.

FINLAND

The Ministry of Education launched a 5-year Information Society Programme in 1995, to promote ICT for teaching and learning in Finnish schools, and to integrate the schools more fully into international networks. A national strategy for the years 2000-2004, relating to education, training and research in the information society, was drawn up in April, 1999, as is briefly outlined below.

First national strategy

The *National Strategy on Education, Training and Research* (Finland, 1995) sought to raise the quality of education and research through ICT, with the underlying goal of guaranteeing equal opportunities to all citizens in the new information environment. The policy addresses the improvement of national competitiveness and employment opportunities, the promotion of basic ICT skills for all, and access to and use of information. The educational priority areas of action are summarised in the following five points, each then developed in somewhat more detail:

- All educational institutions were to have at least ISDN[47]-level Internet connection by the end of 1999.
- National support would be given to educational institutions for purchasing ICT equipment and setting up the technical infrastructure.
- Teachers would be encouraged to use ICT.
- Educational materials would be developed.
- New teaching methods using ICT would be developed.

Connecting and equipping schools

Almost all Finnish schools have applied for state funding to cover half the costs of computers, the balance coming from the schools' governing body, usually the municipality. Equally, nearly all schools are now connected to the Internet,

---

47. ISDN: Integrated Services Digital Network, an international communication standard which provides faster connection than a modem.

the costs of hardware being met on a similar basis. Universities obtained funding directly from the Ministry of Education. The ratio of students per computer in the different phases of education is shown below:

Type of institution	Number of such institutions	Number of students	Students per computer*
Comprehensive school	4 203	591 700	8-10
Upper secondary	430	113 000	6
Vocational, college, polytechnic	361	219 900	3 -5

* Target for 2000.

The professional development of teachers

There are about 100 000 teachers in Finland. Some 65 000 of them are employed in comprehensive and upper secondary schools, vocational education institutions, and on a full-time basis in adult education. The National Board of Education has supported in-service development of teachers' abilities to use ICT, through training sessions lasting five weeks (which counts for 5 credit units, one unit corresponding to 40 hours of study). Teachers can take part once they have demonstrated that they possess the basics of information technology – data processing, e-mail and web browsing skills – together with some pedagogical understanding of the new learning environments. During the first four years, almost 10 000 teachers have participated.

The objective of the in-service provision has been for teachers to become experts in the educational use of ICT and co-operative working methods. There has been an emphasis on whole-school/institution approaches. It has been possible for teachers to participate in the training outside normal school hours, over about half a year, through project work at a distance and contact learning over 8-12 days. Since 1999, the entire course can also be taken over the Internet.

The National Board of Education has spent around EUR 1.5 million annually on this training. In addition, educational institutions have supported in-house staff training for ICT skills, both basic and more specialist. Training programmes have been introduced (three credits) for certain subjects – languages, natural sciences, arts, music, special education, religion and vocational training – with special targetting of. basic ICT skills for teachers more than 50 years old. Programmes and study groups have been organised around the country at universities, continuing education centres and other similar organisations – around 20 organisations in total – the aim being to relate the contact studies as closely as possible to the workplace.

Development of digital learning materials

Since 1996 the National Board of Education has produced about 40 CD-ROMs in Finnish and 6 in Swedish, mostly for biology, mathematics, natural sciences, history and vocational education. Commercial suppliers have also produced some learning materials especially for first-language teaching of Finnish and Swedish, and for the natural sciences. Finland, with a population of only 5 million, has accepted the need to subsidise the production of such learning materials.

Development of new teaching methods

The National Board of Education has part-funded 20 educational projects aimed at developing methods for the integration of ICT into normal classroom teaching. These projects have usually been centred on a co-ordinating school, networked to other schools and universities (especially the teacher training departments or continuing education centres). This model has used brainstorming and critical evaluation, through the contacts that have been made, to develop pedagogical support mechanisms. The projects have developed methodologies for specific subject areas, and for investigative approaches to studying. A couple have focused particularly on disabilities.

The 2000-2004 strategy

We have now entered a national four-year development period, co-ordinated by the Department of Education and Science Policy in the Ministry of Education (Finland, 1999). The overall theme of the strategy, the systematic development of learning environments based on research, can be divided into six sub-themes:
- ICT literacy for all.
- Teachers and other educators to have the necessary ICT skills.
- Professionals in the information and content industries to be informed regarding the educational use of ICT.
- The further development of virtual learning universities and schools.
- Electronic classification and publication of research information and teaching materials.
- Strengthening the structural underpinning of the information society.

This is all working towards a vision that by 2004 Finland will be one of the leading knowledge and information societies. Success will imply all citizens having opportunities to study, to develop their own knowledge, and to make extensive use of information resources and educational services. It will be achieved only through the establishment of a high-quality, ethically and economically sustainable mode of operation in network-based teaching and research.

BIBLIOGRAPHY

AAUW Educational Foundation, Commission on Technology, Gender, and Teacher Education (2000), *Tech-Savvy: Educating Girls in the New Computer Age,* Washington, D.C.

BANGEMANN, M. (1994), *Europe and the Global Information Society: Recommendations to the European Council,* European Union, High-Level Group on the Information Society, Brussels.

BECHT, D., TAGLANG, K. and WILHELM, A. (1999), "The Digital Divide and the US Hispanic Population", *The Digital Beat,* Vol. 1, No. 13 (available on-line: www.benton.org/DigitalBeat/db080699.html).

BECTA (British Educational Communications and Technology Agency) (1998), *Multimedia Portables for Teachers Pilot* (Project Report), Coventry, United Kingdom.

BLOOM, M.R. and LAFLEUR, B. (1999), *Turning Skills into Profit: Economic Benefits of Workplace Education Programs,* The Conference Board, New York (available on-line: http://www.conference-board.org/index.htm).

Boston Globe (1999), Advertisement, 20 October, p. A14.

CAVALLO, D. (1998), MIT Media Lab. (available on-line: www.mit.edu.).

CHAMBERS, J. (1999), quoted in "Next, It's E-ducation", by T. L. Friedman, *New York Times*, 17 November, 1999, p. A29.

CLINTON, W. (2000), *From Digital Divide to Digital Opportunity,* The Whitehouse, Washington, D.C., (available on-line: www.whitehouse.gov/WH/New/digitaldivide/digital1.html).

COFFIELD, F. (1998), *Learning at Work*, The Policy Press, University of Bristol.

CRAWFORD, S. (1999), "Wireless Internet: Coming to a cellphone near you soon", *WOZA Internet (Johannesburg)*, 29 September, distributed via *Africa News Online* (www.africanews.org).

De MOURA CASTRO *et al.* (1999), Mexico's Telesecundaria, September/ October (available on-line: www.TechKnowlLogia.com).

EL BANCO MUNDIAL (1999), *Informe sobre el desarrollo mundial: el conocimiento al servicio del desarrollo*, Madrid.

FIGUERES, J.M. (1999), *Little Intelligent Communities*, General Report, Fundación Costa Rica para el Desarrollo Sostenible.

FINLAND (1995), *Education, Training and Research in the Information Society. A National Strategy for 1996-1999*, Ministry of Education, Helsinki.

FINLAND (1999), *Education, Training and Research in the Information Society. A National Strategy for 2000-2004*, Ministry of Education, Helsinki (available on-line: http://www.minedu.fi/julkaisut/information/englishU/ welcome.html).

FONG, D. (1999), Interview in *Newsweek*, 22 November, p. 104.

FONTAINE, M. and FOOTE, D. (1999), *Ghana: Networking for Local Development: How you can use a computer without owning one. TechKnowlogia*, Vol. 1 (available on-line: http://www.techknowlogia.org).

GEDTS (General Educational Development Testing Service) (1998), *Who took the GED?*, GED 1998 Statistical Report, Washington, D.C.

GIBBS, W.W. (1997), "Taking Computers to Task", *Scientific American*, pp. 82-89, July.

GINSBURG, L. and ELMORE, J. (1998), *Technology in the Workplace: Issues of Workers' Skills* (Technical Report TR98-04), University of Pennsylvania, National Center on Adult Literacy, Philadelphia.

GLADIEUX, L.E. and SWAIL, W.S. (1999), *The Virtual University & Educational Opportunity-Issues of Equity and Access for the Next Generation* (Policy Perspectives), The College Board, Washington, D.C.

GREENE, T.C. (2000), "Disabled People Represent the True Digital Divide", *The Register*, February 22 (available on-line: www.theregister.co.uk).

GROPILLO, C. (1999), *Futura: o Canal do conhecimento*, Ano II – No. 8, Rio de Janeiro.

HAMMOND, A. (1998), *Which World? – Scenarios for the 21st Century: Global Destinies, Regional Choices*, Island Press/Shearwater Books, Washington, D.C.

HATFIELD, D.N. (1997), "Technological Trends in Wireless Telecommunications", prepared in support of a project on "Universal Access", conducted by Gallaudet University for the United States Department of Education (see also www.states.org).

HATIVA, N. (1988), "Computer-based Drill and Practice in Arithmetic: Widening the Gap between High- and Low-Achieving Students", *American Educational Research Journal*, Vol. 25(3), pp. 366-397.

HEALEY, J. (1999), "Giveaway by Cisco aims for share of wireless technology", *Mercury News*, 25 October.

HECKHAUSEN, J. and DWECK, C.S. (1998), *Motivation and Self-Regulation across the Life Span*, Cambridge University Press, Cambridge.

HIRSCH, D. and WAGNER, D.A. (1994), *What Makes Workers Learn?: The Role of Incentives in Workplace Education and Training*, Hampton Press, Cresskill, NJ.

HUNT, T. (1999), "Clinton calls for Sharing Wealth", The Associated Press, November 21.

ITU (1997), "Challenges to the Network: Telecommunications and the Internet", Geneva (see also http://www.itu.int/home).

Japan (1995), *Practical Guidelines for the New Information Age in Education, Science, Sports and culture*, Monbusho, Tokyo.

Japan (1996), *The Model for Japanese Education in the Perspective of the 21st Century*, Monbusho, Tokyo.

Japan (1999), *Information Technology Use in Education Project*, Monbusho, Tokyo.

JONASSEN, D.H., PECK, K.L. and WILSON, B.G. (1999), *Learning with Technology: A Constructivist Perspective*, Merrill, Upper Saddle River, NJ.

KAKU, M. (1997), *Visions: How Science Will Revolutionise the 21st Century*, Anchor Books-Doubleday, New York.

KENDIE, D. (1999), "Africa's Major Obstacles to Development," *Addis Tribune*, 5 November, Addis Ababa, distributed via *Africa News Online* (www.africanews.org.).

KIBATI, M. (1999), "Wireless Local Loop in Developing Countries: Is it Too Soon for Data? – The Case of Kenya", Thesis paper Master of Science in Technology and Policy, p. 10, May, MIT.

KIRSCH, I. S., JUNGBLUT, A., JENKINS, L. and KOLSTAD, A. (1993), *Adult Literacy in America: A first look at the results of the national adult literacy survey* (Report No. 16-PL-02), Educational Testing Service, Princeton, NJ.

LAVIN, B. (1995), "Why the global village cannot afford information slums", in W.J. Drake (ed.), *The New Information Infrastructure: Strategies for United States Policy,* The Twentieth Century Fund Press, New York, p. 205.

MAKOFF, J. (1999), "Motorola to Offer a Chip That Can Support a Variety of Cell-Phone Standards", *New York Times,* 1 November, p. C4.

MANNISTO, L., KELLY, T. and PETRAZZINI, B. (1999), "Internet and the Global Information Infrastructure in Africa", ITU, Geneva.

MELENGA, P. (1999), "Only 0.1% Africans have access to Internet", *The Post of Zambia,* September 9 (distributed via *Africa NewsOnline* www.africanews.org).

MORALES, S. (1997), *Futuro Inteligente. Red de participación ciudadana,* Secretaría de Educación del Distrito, Colombia.

NCES (1999, February) (National Center for Education Statistics), U.S. Department of Education, *Internet Access in Public Schools and Classrooms: 1994-1998* (Issue Brief NCES 99-017) (available online: http://nces.ed.gov/pubs99/1999017.html).

NCES (2000) (National Center for Education Statistics), *Internet Access in U. S. Public Schools and Classrooms: 1994-99* (Stats in Brief, NCES 2000-086), U.S. Department of Education, Office of Educational Research and Improvement.

Neighborhood Networks (1998), *Neighborhood Networks* (available online: http://www.hud.gov/nnw/nnwnbf98.html).

NISPEROS, P.B. (2000, March 13), "Mass Movement Needed to Bridge 'Digital Divide' in Singapore", *K Discussion* (available: www.globalknowledge.org/english/archives/mailarchives/gkd/gkd-mar00/0044.html).

NTIA (National Telecommunications and Information Administration) (1999), *Falling through the Net: Defining the Digital Divide,* U.S. Department of Commerce (available online: http://www.ntia.doc.gov/ntiahome).

OBASI, K. (1999), "Web Without Phones", *The News (Lagos),* November 8 (distributed via *Africa News Online* (www.africanews.org).

OECD/CERI (1999), *Education Policy Analysis 1999,* Paris.

OECD/Statistics Canada (1995), *Literacy, Economy and Society,* Paris.

OECD/Statistics Canada (1997), *Literacy Skills for the Knowledge Society: Further Results from the International Adult Literacy Survey,* Paris.

OECD (2000), *Information Technology Outlook,* Paris.

PAPERT, S. (1997), *The Connected Family, Bridging the Digital Generation Gap,* MIT Media Lab, Long Street Press.

PASTORE, M. (2000), "Crossing the UK's Digital Divide", *InternetNews*, March 30 (available on-line: www.internetnews.co.uk).

PC Magazine (1999), November 16, p. 11 (see http://www.zdnet.com/pcmag/stories/supp/0,7859,2384166,00.html).

Portugal (1996), Ana Benavente (coord.), *A literacia em Portugal – resultados de uma pesquisa extensiva e monografica*, FCG-CNE, Lisbon [see also (2000), *Measuring Adult Literacy – The International Adult Literacy Survey in the European Context*, Office of National Statistics, Great Britain, ch. 13].

Portugal (1997), *Livro Verde para a Sociedade da Informaçao em Portugal,* Missão para a Sociedade da Informação/Ministério da Ciência e Tecnologia, Lisbon (available on-line: http://www.missao-si.mct.pt).

Portugal (1998), "Education, integration, citizenship: policy guideline document for basic education", Ministry of Education, Lisbon.

Portugal (2000*a*), *Programa do XIV Governo Constitucional – Apresentação e Debate*, Assembleia da República, Lisbon.

Portugal (2000*b*), PRODEP III (2000-2006) – Ministério da Educação, Ministério do Planeamento.

RUSSELL, M. (1999), "Testing on Computers: A Follow-up Study Comparing Performance on Computer and on Paper", *Education Policy Analysis Archives,* Vol. 7(20) (available on-line: epaa.asu.edu/epaa/v7n20).

SCANS (Secretary's Commission on Achieving Necessary Skills, U.S. Department of Labor) (1991), *What Work Requires of Schools: A SCANS report for America 2000,* U.S. Government Printing Office, Washington, D.C.

SCHOFIELD, J.W. and DAVIDSON, A.L. (1998), *The Internet and Equality of Educational Opportunity,* Paper presented at the World Conference on ED-MEDIA/ED-TELECOM, June, Freiberg, Germany.

SCHUNK, D.H. and ZIMMERMAN, B.J. (1994), *Self-Regulation of Learning and Performance: Issues and Educational Applications,* Erlbaum, Hillsdale, NJ.

Secretaría de Educación Pública (1999), *Perfil de la educación en México,* Comisión Nacional de los Libros de Texto Gratuitos, Mexico.

STEWART, T.A. (1997), *Intellectual Capital: The New Wealth of Organizations*, Nicholas Brealey Publishing, London.

Strategis Group (1999), as reported in *USA Today*, November 30.

STRAUSS, C. (1998), *Assistive Devices for Use With Personal Computers,* National Library Service for the Blind and Physically Handicapped, Library of Congress, Washington, D.C.

Sweden (1991), *Växa med kunskaper* (Government Bill: Growing with Knowledge) (prop. 1990/91:85).

Sweden (1996), *Vissa åtgärder för att halvera arbetslösheten till år 2000* (Government Bill: Certain Measures in order to Halve the Unemployment) (prop. 1995/96:222).

Sweden (1998*a*), *Lärandets verktyg – nationellt program för IT i skolan* (Tools for Learning – A National Programme for ICT in Schools) (skr. 1997/98:176).

Sweden (1998*b*), SIKA (Statens Institut för KommunikationsAnalys/SCB), *Kommunikationsundersökningen 1998* (KOM98) (Communications Survey).

Sweden (1998*c*), *Regional tillväxt – för arbete och välfärd* (Government Bill: Regional Growth – for Work and Welfare) (prop. 1997/98:62).

Sweden (1998*d*), "Facts about Sweden – Adult Education", Swedish Institute, May.

Sweden (1998*e*), *Informationstekniken i skolan, en forskningsöversikt* (Information and Communication Technology in Schools, a Research Overview), Pedersen, National Agency for Education.

Sweden (1999*a*), *Budgetpropositionen för 2000* (Government Budget Bill for 2000) (prop. 1999/2000:1).

Sweden (1999*b*), *Kvalitetsutvecklingen i svensk barnomsorg och skola 1999* (The Development of Quality in Swedish Child Care and School 1999), National Agency for Education.

Sweden (1999*c*), *Samverkan, ansvar och utveckling – utvecklingsplan för förskola, skola och vuxenutbildning* (National Development Plan for Pre-school, School and Adult Education) (skr. 1998/99:121).

Sweden (1999*d*), *Skolans datorer 1999,* Skolverket rapport nr 176 (Computers at school 1999, National Agency for Education report number 176).

Sweden (1999*e*), *Datoranändningen ökar men stora grupper står fortfarande utanför* (The Use of Computers is Increasing but Large Groups are still Excluded), Landsorganisationen (LO), November.

Sweden (1999*f*), *Kvalificerad yrkesutbildning* (Advanced Vocational Education), (SOU 1999:122) Swedish Government Commission.

Sweden (2000), *Ett informationssamhälle för alla* (Government Bill: An Information Society for Everybody) (prop. 1999/2000:86).

Technology Front (1999), "A bit-cloud above the city", Source: Tasty Bits From the Technology Front (see http://www.tbtf.com).

The World Bank (1998), *World Development Indicators, 1998*, CD-ROM, Washington, D.C., 1.2.

The World Bank (1999), *World Development Report 1999/2000: Entering the 21st Century*, Washington, D.C.

TRIPLETT, J.E. (1998), *The Solow Productivity Paradox: What do Computers do to Productivity?* (Review Paper), Centre for the Study of Living Standards, Ottawa, ON.

TUIJNMAN, A., KIRSCH, I. and WAGNER, D.A. (1997), *Adult Basic Skills: Innovations in Measurement and Policy Analysis,* Hampton Press, Cresskill, NJ.

United Kingdom (1998*a*), "Our Information Age: overall UK government strategy on the new technologies", London.

United Kingdom (1998*b*), "Open for Learning, Open for Business: policy statement and challenge to industry on the development of the National Grid for Learning", London.

United Kingdom (2000), "Closing the Digital Divide", report of Policy Action Team 15, DTI, London (available on-line: http://www.pat15.org.uk).

UNESCO (1998), *Informe Mundial sobre la Educación: Los docentes y la enseñanza en un mundo en mutación*, Santillana, Madrid.

UNICEF (1999), *The State of the World's Children: Education,* New York.

WAGNER, D.A. (1995), "Literacy and development: Rationales, myths, innovations, and future directions", *International Journal of Educational Development*, Vol. 15, pp. 341-362.

WAGNER, D.A. (2000), "Literacy and Adult Education", *Global Thematic Review,* World Education Forum (Dakar), UNESCO, Paris.

WAGNER, D.A.. and VENEZKY, R.L. (1999), "Adult literacy: The next generation", *Educational Researcher*, 28, 1, pp. 21-29.

WAGNER, D.A., VENEZKY, R.L. and STREET, B.V. (1999), *Literacy: An International Handbook*, Westview Press, Boulder, CO.

OECD PUBLICATIONS, 2, rue André-Pascal, 75775 PARIS CEDEX 16
PRINTED IN FRANCE
(96 2000 08 1 P 1) ISBN 92-64-18288-8 – No. 51485 2000